GYPSY

This book unve[...]
tunetelling, explainin[...]
methods used by these nomads. For generations
they have survived on their skills as seers. Their
accuracy is lengendary. They are a people who
seem to be born with "the sight" . . . the ability to
look into the past, present and future using only the
simplest of tools to aid them.

Here you will learn to read palms, to interpret
the symbols in a teacup, to read cards . . . both the
Tarot and regular playing cards. Here are revealed
the secrets of interpreting the actions of animals, of
reading the weather, of recognizing birthmarks and
the shape of hands. You may divine the future with
dice, with dominoes, with knives, needles and sticks.
You can impress your friends with your knowledge
of many of these lesser Mysteries; uncommon forms
of fortunetelling known only to a few.

The methods of divination presented in this
book are all *practical* methods—no expensive or
hard-to-get items are necessary. The Gypsies are
accomplished at using natural objects and everyday
items to serve them in their endeavors. Sticks and
stones, knives and needles, cards and dice . . . some
are found along the roadside, or in the woods,
others are easily obtainable at little expense from
the village store, the five-and-dime, the con-
venience store, or the traveling peddler.

Using these non-complex objects, and following the traditional Gypsy ways shown, you can
become a seer and improve the quality of your own
life and of those lives around you.

ABOUT THE AUTHOR

Ray Buckland's grandfather was the first of the Buckland Gypsies to give up traveling the roads in a wagon and to settle in a permanent house. From his earliest years Ray remembers listening to his father's and grandfather's tales of Romani life, and watching his grandmother read cards and tell fortunes. This early upbringing instilled in him a deep respect for the Old Ways. From his teens, Ray Buckland started his own serious studies of the Old Knowledge, and later, came to write about it in a number of best-selling books. "Buckland" is a well-known name among English Gypsies, and Ray Buckland has become a well-known author of books on practical magic. He is today regarded as one of the leading authorities on witchcraft, voodoo and the supernatural.

To Write to the Author

We cannot guarantee that every letter written to the author can be answered, but all will be forwarded. Both the author and the publisher appreciate hearing from readers, learning of your enjoyment and benefit from this book. Llewellyn also publishes a bi-monthly news magazine with news and reviews of practical esoteric studies and articles helpful to the student, and some readers' questions and comments to the author may be answered through this magazine's columns if permission to do is included in the original letter. The author sometimes participates in seminars and workshops, and dates and places are announced in *The Llewellyn New Times*. To write to the author, or to ask a question, write to:

Raymond Buckland
c/o THE LLEWELLYN NEW TIMES
P.O. Box 64383-051, St. Paul, MN 55164-0383, U.S.A.

Please enclose a self-addressed, stamped envelope for reply, or $1.00 to cover costs.

ABOUT LLEWELLYN'S NEW AGE SERIES

The "New Age"—it's a phrase we use, but what does it mean? Does it mean that we are entering the Aquarian Age? Does it mean that a new Messiah is coming to correct all that is wrong and make Earth into a Garden? Probably not—but the idea of a *major change* is there, combined with awareness that Earth *can* be a Garden; that war, crime, poverty, disease, etc., are not necessary "evils."

Optimists, dreamers, scientists . . . nearly all of us believe in a "better tomorrow," and that somehow we can do things now that will make for a better future life for ourselves and for coming generations.

In one sense, we all know there's nothing new under the Heavens, and in another sense that every day makes a new world. The difference is in our consciousness. And this is what the New Age is all about: it's a major change in consciousness found within each of us as we learn to bring forth and manifest powers that Humanity has always potentially had.

Evolution moves in "leaps." Individuals struggle to develop talents and powers, and their efforts build a "power bank" in the Collective Unconsciousness, the soul of Humanity that suddenly makes these same talents and powers easier access for the majority.

You still have to learn the "rules" for developing and applying these powers, but it is more like a "relearning" than a *new* learning, because with the New Age it is as if the basis for these had become genetic.

Books by Raymond Buckland

Practical Candleburning Rituals
Witchcraft from the Inside
Witchcraft . . . the Religion
A Pocket Guide to the Supernatural
Witchcraft Ancient and Modern
Here is the Occult
The Tree: Complete Book of Saxon Witchcraft
The Magic of Chant-O-Matics
Anatomy of the Occult
Practical Color Magick
Buckland's Complete Book of Witchcraft

with Hereward Carrington

Amazing Secrets of the Psychic World

under the pseudonym "Tony Earll"

Mu Revealed

Forthcoming by Raymond Buckland

Gypsy Fortunetelling Deck
Gypsy Love Magick
Gypsy Dream Reading
Gypsy Spells and Charms

Llewellyn's New Age Series

Secrets of
Gypsy
Fortunetelling

Raymond Buckland

1988
Llewellyn Publications
St. Paul, Minnesota, 55164-0383, U.S.A.

International Standard Book Number: 0-87542-051-6
Library of Congress Catalog Number: 88-45196

First Edition, 1988
First Printing, 1988

Library of Congress Cataloging-in-Publication Data
Buckland, Raymond.
Secrets of gypsy fortunetelling.

(Llewellyn's new age series)
1. Divination—History.   2. Gypsies—History.
I. Title.   II. Series.
BF1751.B83   1988   133.3'08991497   88-45196
ISBN 0-87542-051-6 (pbk.)

Photos: Raymond Buckland

Produced by Llewellyn Publications
Typography and Art property of Chester-Kent, Inc.

Published by
LLEWELLYN PUBLICATIONS
A Division of Chester-Kent, Inc.
P.O. Box 64383
St. Paul, MN 55164-0383, U.S.A.
Printed in the United States of America

For my parents and grandparents
—Stanley and Lizzie Buckland;
Bert and Alice Buckland—
and for all Buckland Travelers

CONTENTS

INTRODUCTION

I am what is known as a *poshrat* or half-blood Romani (from *posh*—half; *ratti*—blood). My father was a full-blood. My grandfather was the first of the family to settle into a permanent dwelling and give up the traveling ways *jalling a drom* in a *vardo*. There are old photographs of Buckland Gypsies and their waggons in such books as *The Gypsies—Waggon-Time and After* by Denis Harvey, *The English Gypsy Caravan* by C.H. Ward-Jackson and Denis E. Harvey, and in *Making Model Gypsy Caravans* by John Thompson. Charles Godfrey Leland also mentions a Buckland Gypsy in his *Gypsy Fortune-Telling and Magic*.

To many, the Gypsies have always seemed a mysterious people, mainly because they tend to keep very much to themselves and have a distrust of *gaujos*, or non-Gypsies. The Gypsies—or, to give them their true name, the *Rom* (Romani)—have always been well versed in occult lore and have been particularly adept at divination, or fortunetelling. Indeed, they were responsible for bringing with them much of our present knowledge of this field, in their migration from the East, and through their travels have spread this knowledge.

One of the things that has helped keep the Rom insulated from the many peoples and countries through which they have traveled is language. They have their own language: *Romanes*. It has certainly changed over the centuries, and in different countries many local words have been picked up and added to it. But the basics have remained enough that a Gypsy from one country can usually manage to talk with a Gypsy from any other country. The Rom words I include in this book are English Romanes, or *poggerdi jib*.

There are many Sanskrit words, or words derived from Sanskrit, in Romanes, which is another indication of the origin of the Rom.

Dukkerin' is the Romani word for fortunetelling (there is an older word, *drabbering*, but that is not used, or even much known, today). Although literally meaning "hand reading" (*duk*=hand), *dukkering'* is used for all forms of divination: reading palms, cards and tea leaves, throwing dice, crystal gazing, interpreting omens and portents. Whatever its form, however, *dukkerin'* is of a PRACTICAL nature in that the Gypsy utilizes nothing more complex than, for example, a deck of cards, a cup of tea, a bunch of sticks, or a set of dice—all easily obtainable items of no great worth in themselves.

My grandfather read palms and was an expert at interpreting the actions of birds and animals. My grandmother—a true *shuvani* (Wise Woman)— favored the cards. Both were very psychic themselves and could function well without any tools, yet they both knew that "props" can be useful. Basically they serve as a focal point and as a means of graphically illustrating what needs to be emphasized . . . turn over the "Death" card in a tarot deck and you'll really capture the attention of the person you're reading for!

The Gypsies, more than any other people, were responsible for the interest in, and perfection of, the divinatory arts, promoting them and spreading them—as the Gypsies themselves spead—across Asia and Europe then into the New World. Let's look for a moment at the history of these travelers.

THE COMING OF
THE GYPSIES

Somewhere around the mid-ninth century a large group of people left their homeland in the north of India and moved Westward. What prompted this initial move we do not know, but it was the start of a wave of dark-skinned nomads that grew in number and swarmed across Asia and Europe.

According to Petulengro:

> . . . through Afghanistan and Persia they came, reaching the Caspian Sea (to the north of the Persian Gulf). They had split into different bands earlier. The northern tribe went up the Euphrates and Tigris. Then some went to the Black Sea and others to Syria, but the majority went to Turkey. Another tribe went through Palestine and Egypt. The southern group went along the north Africa coast until they came to Gibraltar and crossed into Spain. The branch that passed through Turkey crossed the Bosporus, into Greece and the Balkans, and from there into Central Europe.

By 1417 there were Gypsies in Germany; by 1430 they had reached England.

By the time they reached western Europe, the Gypsies carried with them seemingly authentic "Letters of Protection" from various rulers, including Sigismund, King of the Romans (actually King of Hungary) and even Pope Martin V. On the basis of these letters, initially they were generally well received. It was a time when the Church had elevated charity into a virtue, so charity was universally extended to these colorful vagrants.

Various stories circulated concerning the travelers. A common one was that they were living out a seven year penance imposed on them because of their paganism. However, they would temporarily settle in an area and happily live off the sympathetic charity for many times the seven years. They gradually came to be regarded as part of the so-called "dangerous classes." Jean-Paul Clébert (in *Les Tsiganes*) quotes the "General Inventory of the History of Thieves" that said:

> ". . . to be considered as an outstanding robber, it was necessary to have passed through (or graduated from) the 'Beggars' Republic'; to know all the tricks and wiles and activities of the Gypsies; to be acquainted with the various groups within that organization . . ."

This was the beginning of the persecutions from which the Gypsy people still have not freed themselves.

The sudden arrival of thousands of these people was enough to cause consternation in many of the countries they "invaded." They became a major social problem. In much of the West, the reaction was persecution. King Ferdinand of Spain was the first to take specific action. In 1492 he banished Gypsies. Any who would not leave were to be exterminated. Again to quote Clébert:

> People of fixed residence, at one and the same time suspicious and credulous, regarded all those of itinerant occupations who had no settled abode and came from distant countries as possessed of the evil eye . . . every stranger was suspect; all the more if he had a swarthy face, wore rings in his ears, lived in 'wheeled houses', and spoke a language which was obviously not a Christian one."

The Gypsies were equated with Witches and Sorcerers. They were accused of engaging in black magick and dealing with the Devil. The Parliament of Paris, in 1539, recorded an expulsion order and in 1560 the States General of Orléans called on "all those imposters known by the name of Bohemians or Egyptians to leave the kingdom under penalty of the galleys." In 1607 Henri IV renewed the expulsion order.

But in fact these expulsion orders had small effect and the Gypsies continued practicing their crafts, albeit under a state of persecution. This persecution has continued through to the present. In the Second World War, almost half a million Gypsies were gassed, shot or hanged in the Nazi concentration camps, yet this is today seldom remembered or remarked upon.

In Britain and America the Gypsies continue to be hounded and their nomadic lifestyle is looked upon as somehow antagonistic to "the system." But the Gypsies, the *Rom,* doggedly refuse to conform. They see no reason to be forced to change their life-style of centuries if they can possibly get away with it. They continue to *jal a drom* (travel the road) as wandering peddlers, musicians, dancers, dealers in all things, and tellers-of-fortunes. I hope they always will.

Square Bow-Top Style Vardo

DUKKERIN'

Among the Gypsies there are four favorites for dukkerin'. They are: the palm, tea leaves, the crystal, and cards (not neccessarily in that order). I'll look at these first and then go on to some of the other methods employed, including several that are little known in the world of the *gaujo*, or non-Gypsy.

One thing needs to be kept in mind when doing readings. That is, that most people do take them seriously. Even those who outwardly profess to laugh at the very idea of being able to see any indication of future events do, unconsciously perhaps, take your words to heart. Because of this you should be very careful in what you say. For example, if you should see death in your client's future, do *not* say "Oh! You're going to die!" Always choose your words carefully, stressing the necessity to be extra careful or to pay particular attention to their health at certain times, rather than boldly stating that there will be an accident or that they will suffer some dreadful disease. As much as possible, try to stress la Clero fe.

the *good* things. Don't forget that we create our own realities; that what you see indicated in the cards, the palm, or wherever, is only an indication of what is likely to happen with the forces currently in play. The future *can* be changed. We do have freedom of choice. If, then, you stress the favorable aspects, you will set the person's mind toward creating what he or she really wants to happen. The rest is then up to them.

One further point—it is quite possible, and permissible, to read for yourself. Yes, you can read your own palm, your own cards, your own tea leaves, etc. There is nothing wrong in that at all. You may well tend to read into it things that you are aware of, or things that you would like to see (wishful thinking), and to ignore those things you don't want to see! However, by reading on a regular basis you will be able to overcome this tendency to a large extent. So, don't listen to anyone who says that you can't, or shouldn't, read for yourself.

HAND READING

The Gypsy palmist is always an attraction, whether at carnivals, "tea rooms" or through chance encounter—always the center of attention. Using the palm of the hand as a focal point, the Gypsy palmist can tell all of your past, present and future with seemingly uncanny accuracy. Is there a trick to this? No. The only "trick" is in learning the meanings of the various lines, mounts, divisions and types of hand.

GENERAL OBSERVATIONS

What makes the lines in your hands? It's the way in which we use them. The major lines of the hands are caused by the folding of the palm and the activity of the fingers. The heavy, resisting hand will be less lined than the flexible one, and so also will "heavy" natures be less influenced by others and by surroundings than will more delicate natures.

What determines *type?* The makeup of the whole body gives the type of hand. We seldom see hands completely at variance with the rest of the body, though it can happen on occasion. An example would be the "inherited" hand . . . much as we find a family nose, or family jaw, so can we find a family hand. Another exception is the person who keeps a very conscious division between his actual desires and aptitudes and his place in the world. Such a person is either leading a double life or is so secretive that it amounts to a mania (such secretive people must be consciously or unconsciously aware that their hands give them away and instinctively tend to keep their hands tightly closed, as though in an effort to hide their palms).

The hand is individual at birth and changes with life's vicissitudes. The condition of the palm reveals a great deal. Nervousness, for example, shows itself in several ways: an over-moist palm, or a super-dry one; or it has a spottiness—an underskin seemingly patched by dark and light dots.

The hand that is cold and dry needs attention; the circulation is imperfect. If it is hot and dry the nerves need relaxing (intestinal disorders often show up this way).

The knottiness of rheumatism shouldn't be mistaken for the heavy joints of temper. The former is nubby; the latter has a more even thickness at the joint.

I have talked with many Gypsies on the subject of palm reading. The following is a compilation of all they have told me.

THE OUTLINE, FINGERS AND MOUNTS

Short Hands

Short hands generally indicate a tendency to

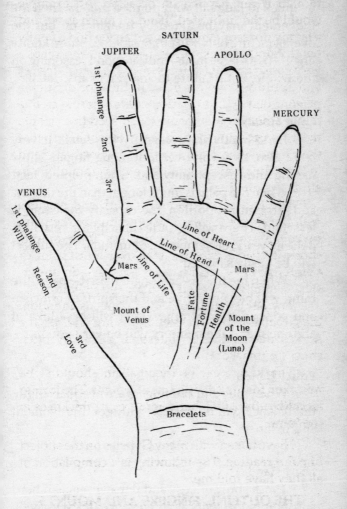

be quick to judge. If with pointed fingers, then the judgement may be aided by imagination but the overall picture only will be considered. Short, knotty fingers (with large joints) indicate good reasoning on the whole, but a failure to analyze in any detail.

Long Hands

Long hands show capacity for detail. If very large also, they will overdo it. Long fingers show feeling and susceptibility and, when pointed, tact.

When the palm is much longer than the fingers, and large in proportion, the capacity for detail is lessened. There will be little capacity for very fine, delicate work, either mental or manual. The subject will be easily satisfied.

When the fingers are longer than the palm, the mind will be very active and the spirit of criticism and contradiction strong. There will be a love of argument and the memory will be very good.

Equal Hands

When the palm and fingers are of equal length, the balance will be perfect, with good judgement and instinct.

Hard Hands

These show energy and perseverance. If hard and pointed, activity with elegance. If excessively hard, however, there is an indication of some lack of intelligence.

Soft Hands

These show laziness of mind and/or body. Soft and spatulate indicate an active mind but a lazy body; soft and square, the reverse. It should be noted, however, that here there is nothing to do with the skin. That may be hardened by the subject's occupation or softened by lack of manual labor. The softness of the hand here dealt with is a judgement based on the *consistency* when pressed.

Supple fingers show quick action and versatility. Very thick hands show selfishness and self-esteem.

Skin

When the hand is soft and the skin very lined, the subject will be impressionable. If hard and lined, quarrelsome. All hands covered with many small lines show either an agitated life or ill health. A very white hand, which does not change with heat and cold, is a sign of selfishness.

Nails

The nails, and the ends of the fingers, show the temper of the subject (the lines have also to be considered, but more on that below). Short and square nails show a fighting temper. If wider than they are long, obstinacy. If square at the bottom instead of curved, passionate anger. Short nails, even with a hand otherwise benevolent, show criticism and contradiction.

Very large nails, curved at the bottom, indicate a good head for business. If they flush pink at the outer edges, there may be occasional fits of irritation.

Thin nails are an indication of delicate health.

When nails are ridged and hard there is a condition of health that needs looking into; it might be undernourishment or intestinal disorder. Bad circulation will produce a blueness. Hard and brittle nails show a lack of oil and mineral salts in the system.

FINGERS

The fingers are generally divided into three classes: pointed, square and spatulate (the class is more easily judged from looking at the back of the hand rather than the front). Sometimes you will find a mixture, for example a hand with a pointed first finger and the others square. For this reason let's look at each of the fingers (and thumb) separately.

The phalanges of the fingers are counted from the top—the first phalange being the one with the nail.

Thumb

The thumb is the most important feature of the whole hand, the character of the subject depending to a great deal on it.

> 1st Phalange: Will
> 2nd Phalange: Reason
> 3rd Phalange: Love

First Phalange. Long and strong = energetic will, self confidence, love of perfection. A person of will. Medium = passive resistance. Short = changeableness, inconsistency.

Second Phalange. This should be a little longer than the first and should be rather thick. When the first and second are of the same length, and the thumb is relatively longer than the other fingers, it indicates a very strong and sensible character. If the same thumb is only of medium length, there will be no rule over others but passive resistance and a strong and wise character. With the first phalange short and the second long and thick, the character will be reasonable but liable to indecision. A good strong first phalange with a long thick second may lead to success and fortune.

Third Phalange. This is also called the Mount of Venus and will be further discussed as that below. If very thick and high, encroaching onto the middle of the hand, the subject will be governed by passion. If medium and in harmony with the rest of the hand, affectionate and benevolent. If weak and flat, cold-hearted and (unless the Heart line is good) selfish.

A thumb too short shows indecisiveness. If wide and heavy at the point it will indicate obstinacy, particularly if the joint is knotty. The wider the phalange, the more pig-headed the subject! If the thumb bends inwards towards the fingers it indicates avarice. If it bends outwards it's a sign of generosity and, sometimes, extravagance. If it is straight, it means prudence and good sense. A thumb set low on the hand shows talent.

First Finger. The finger of Jupiter, and the finger of Justice.

This should be long relative to the other fingers and it should be straight.

Pointed indicates quick apprehension, intuition, love of reading.

Square—love of truth.

Spatulate—(very rare) error, exaggerated action.

If Pointed when the other fingers are Square, serious thought and artistic talent.

First Phalange relatively long—religion.

Second Phalange relatively long—ambition.

Third Phalange relatively long—pride; love of rule.

All short—want of thought; little contemplation.

Second Finger. The finger of Saturn, and the finger of Success.

Pointed—Frivolity, carelessness.

Square—Prudence, grave character, sadness.

Spatulate—Activity, superstition.

First Phalange relatively long—melancholy.

Second Phalange relatively long—love of agriculture.

Third Phalange relatively long—avarice.

Third Finger. The finger of Apollo, and the finger of Art, Fame and Riches.

Pointed—Artistic feeling and intuition. If with all of the others in opposition—frivolity and boasting.

Square—Truth and reason in art and in life.

Spatulate—Love of form, of movement in art, dramatic talent. Many actors have this finger and in artists it signifies painters of animal or genre subjects.

First Phalange relatively long—love of art and color.

Second Phalange relatively long—love of work.

> Third Phalange relatively long—love of display, vanity, desire to shine, love of riches.

Fourth Finger. The finger of Mercury, and the finger of affection.

> It is good that this finger should be straight and long, and if the subject would "turn others around his little finger" then it should rise above the first knot of the third finger.

> *Pointed*—Eloquence, tact, diplomacy. There is, however, a leaning towards trickery if excessively pointed.

> *Square*—Reason in science, love of the abstract, good at teaching, good at business.

> *Spatulate*—Mechanical skill, love of machinery. If excessively spatulate it indicates a tendency towards theft.

> First Phalange relatively long—love of talking, eloquence, skill.

> Second Phalange relatively long—industry, common sense, good at business, love of argument.

> Third Phalange relatively long—scheming, lying.

If, when the hands are held open and loose, the first and second fingers fall naturally widest apart, it shows independence of thought. If the third and fourth are widest, independence of action. If both are very wide, great originality and self-reliance. If the fingers naturally curl up towards the palm when so held, the subject will be conventional.

When the third phalanges of all fingers are thick at the root, it is a sign of greediness or, at least, of a love of good things to eat and drink. When the third phalanges of all the fingers incline downwards below the mounts, it shows shyness and, sometimes, extreme cowardice. If the first phalanges hollow and curve upwards—avarice. Reversed—extravagance.

Thumb inclined inwards—avarice and selfishness; outwards—generosity.

It should be noted that the inclination of the fingers towards each other requires a lot of study. No one seems to have studied this aspect sufficiently. The few rules outlined above are the ones used by most Romani, but it seems there is still much to be learned on this point.

THE MOUNTS

As with the lines, the meaning of the mounts (lying at the base of the fingers and thumb) may be modified by other indications in the hand. The qualities listed are those associated with that particular mount. If the mount seems especially full and fleshy, then consider the listing "Excess." If, however, the mount seems especially flat and lacking in flesh, then consider the listing "Absence."

Mount of Jupiter (first finger)
Qualities: Religion, ambition, honor, gaiety, love of society.

A good Mount of Jupiter will always show a great mind.

> Excess—Pride, love of power, domineering, conceit, superstitious.
>
> Absence—Irreligious, selfishness, idleness, want of dignity, vulgarity.

Mount of Saturn (second finger)
Qualities: Prudence, wisdom.

> Excess—Taciturnity, sadness, love of solitude.
>
> Absence—Misfortune, insignificance in life.

Mount of Apollo (third finger)
Qualities: Love of art or literature, genius, intelligence, hope, calm, beauty and grace of mind, gentleness, toleration, mercy.

> Excess—Love of money, extravagance, curiosity, boasting, scoffing, lying, envy.
>
> Absence—Dullness, insignificance.

Mount of Mercury (fourth finger)
Qualities: Cheerfulness, intelligence, wit, eloquence, industry, inventiveness, promptness of action and thought, love of work.

> Excess—Lying, theft, treachery, ruse, trickery, pretentiousness, ignorance.
>
> Absence—Want of intelligence and aptitude, negativity.

Mount of Mars
There are two Mounts of Mars. One is beneath the Mount of Jupiter, divided from it by the Line of Life, and the other is beneath the Mount of Mercury,

divided from it by the Line of Heart. The Plain of Mars lies between the two.

Qualities of the first (beneath Jupiter): Active, courage, presence of mind, resolution, aggressiveness.

> Excess—great courage, dash and daring, love of danger for its own sake.

> Absence—Cowardice, timidity, want of presence of mind.

Qualities of the second (beneath Mercury): Passive courage, devotion, self-command, resignation, strength of resistance, noble pride.

> Excess—Great fortitude, calm strength, power of forgiveness.

> Absence—Cowardice, timidity, want of presence of mind.

Note: For both Mounts, when the Excess is together with negative lines, it can mean cruelty, tyranny, blood-thirstiness, anger, injustice, insolence, so study these Mounts very carefully and read them in conjunction with the lines (as you should do with all Mounts, of course).

Mount of Venus (thumb)

Qualities: Beauty, grace, affection, charity, benevolence, love of beautiful things, of dancing, of melody in music, desire of pleasing, and the pleasures of the senses.

> Excess—Inconstancy, effrontery, coquetry, vanity, idleness, sensuality.

> Absence—Coldness, selfishness, want of tenderness and love.

Note: If the Mount is flat, there is a want of the

qualities. With a hard hand, a much-developed Mount will give wit and grace of manner, and will counteract the melancholy of a developed Mount of Saturn.

Mount of Luna

This is found on the outside of the hand, beneath the Mount of Mars and opposite that of Venus.
Qualities: Imagination, sentiment, refinement, poetry, harmony in music, love of scenery.

> Excess—Despair, discontent, caprice, irritability, sadness, supersitition.
> Absence—Dullness, want of sympathy, of imagination, of ideas, severe judgement of others.

The mounts should always be judged with due regard for the shape of the fingers, otherwise there is a danger of confusing positive and negative qualities. It is also very necessary to study and understand the lines. For example, a straight Line of Head, a poor Line of Heart, knotted fingers, and a long first phalange of the thumb will give to a fine Line of Apollo love of money instead of art; the subject will be a speculator, not an artist. Look also to see if idleness (soft hand) will not prevent success. Look also to see if the Mounts inclined towards each other. If Mercury encroaches on Apollo, science will join art; if towards the "percussion" or outside of the hand, it will show a talent for business. Mars inclining towards Mercury will denote courage in free speech, and energy in the management of affairs. Mars towards Luna; energy in imagination, and so on.

TIME

Time is counted downwards on the Line of Life, and also downwards on the Line of Head. On the Line of Fate, on the contrary, time is counted upwards from the wrist to the Mount of Saturn. This is also the case with the Line of Fortune. On the Line of Heart it is counted from the Mount of Jupiter to the percussion of the hand.

THE LINES

Line of Life (Vital)

The Line of Life concerns itself literally with the matter of physical being. It extends around the thumb at the place where the thumb of a glove would be sewn on.

The Line of Life shows the length of the subject's existence and his health or illness during the period. Time is measured on it and the incidents marked on the other lines are corroborated.

The Line of Life should be long, narrow, deep, softly colored and completely encircling the Mount of Venus. This will indicate long life, without illness, and a good character.

Signs of illness; Line pale and very deep: bad health. Small dark clots on it: nervous illness. Small lines crossing it: small illnesses, generally headaches. Chained and uneven: painful life, bad health. Stopping suddenly with a dark dot: death by accident or violence. Broken in one hand and weak in the other:

a serious illness. Broken in both hands: probabl death. Forked at the end: possible insanity—wher this is found it is good to caution the subject agains overwork, either mentally or physically. It is alway a bad sign and a serious warning.

Branches: When branch lines rise on either side of th Line of Life, it shows riches and dignity; if they fa downwards it indicates poverty or loss of characte If the Life Line is divided and one branch goes awa onto the Mount of Luna and deepens, it shows lon voyages and distant traveling. Cross lines—Man very small cross lines: ill health and delicate con stitution. Lines from the Mount of Venus crossin the Line of Life are misfortunes caused by othe people.

Attendant lines: When the Line of Life is closel followed by another line, which may occasionall intertwine itself with it, it's a sign of great vigor anc success and a promise of riches. Lines further of from the Line of Life, which follow its course more or less regularly, represent the influence of othe people over the subject's life. Their intensity anc duration may be calculated by their depths and b the nearness of their approach to the Line of Life.

Stars and Crosses: Near the Line of Life, these car indicate trouble. It is often an infirmity from which the subject may not recover. When the Vital Line ends in a series of crosses, the subject may have ar amiable character and talent but if the crosses are found in both hands, he will never succeed in anything great in his life.

Line of Head (Cerebral)

Should be even, long and narrow. This will show strong judgement, determined will, and clear mind. If the Mount of Mercury is much developed, there will be originality and energy. If Mercury is low, more learning and less ability.

When the line is separated from the Line of Life, this is a sign of self-confidence and, when found in both hands, sometimes conceit. Such subjects can be impulsive and should be warned against acting hastily.

When the Line of Head is joined to the Line of Life, this is a sign of a need for self-confidence. If it is joined as far as the middle of both hands, timidity and moral cowardice will be excessive. Unless there are signs of very great talent, such subjects will never succeed at anything.

When the line is very long and straight, this is a sign of common sense, of care and economy. If it goes straight, right across the hand, however, it indicates avarice, selfishness and greed. But this need not be the case if the other signs are very good in the hand—with a fine Mount of Jupiter, a turned-out thumb, and a good Line of Heart.

When the line is very long and sloping, this is a sign of imagination, artistic feeling, poetry, but little judgement. In excess it will bring much folly and delusion, especially if the Mount of Luna is much developed and lined.

When the Line of Head is forked, this is a good sign. In fact it is a good sign for any line to be forked, with the exception of the Line of Life. When the Head Line ends in a small fork, it shows both imagination and common sense. Should the fork be large, it indicates a tendency to trickery and/or diplomacy! The subject may deceive himself, but he also has the ability to deceive others.

When the line is short, and only advances to the middle of the hand, it shows a want of spirit, dash and balance. The subject will see only one side of any question. If it stops under the Mount of Saturn, life will be short and death sudden.

When the line is chained, it shows a want of fixity in ideas; there is too much variety. But if the line is followed throughout by another, sister line, it often indicates a great inheritance.

Line of Heart (Mensal)

This should be narrow and deep, of a good color, and running straight from the Mount of Jupiter to the Mount of Mercury. This indicates a good heart; strong and happy affection. The longer the Heart Line, the nobler and more ideal the love. But should the line completely encircle the Mount of Jupiter, and the Head Line slope on Luna, the subject may make himself unhappy with jealousy.

When the line is short, not rising until beneath the Mount of Saturn, it is a sign of a cold heart. With a very long Head Line and strong thumb, the subject will be very constant, even though the Heart Line is short. This will make him affectionate to the few he loves, though lacking in general love to his fellow-men.

When the line is forked, a fork under Jupiter is a true sign of trustworthiness and constancy, but not of happiness in love. The more even the fork, the more ideal the character.

Branches rising and falling from the Line of Heart show the influence of other people on the affections. A branch that rises high on the Mount of Jupiter promises great happiness and successful ambition, if uncrossed. When a branch cuts through the line and descends beneath it, it is a sign of disappointment. When there are many branches it is a sign that the feelings of love and hate are very strong. No branches mean a loveless life so far as the opposite sex is concerned.

A break in the Line of Heart generally means a broken engagement, or great disappointment with regard to a person loved.

Dots and dents on the Heart Line show troubles, both physical and mental. When the dot is red, the sorrow has been very keen. White dots are conquests in love. Black or blue ones are signs of shock or illness.

When the line is chained, or has islands, it indicates inconstancy, caprice, flirtation, and intrigue. It sometimes indicates even contempt for the opposite sex.

Line of Fate (Saturnian)

This shows worldly success or failure, and the general course of the life. There are four principal places for the departure of this line:

i. From the Line of Life: This is good and common. The line then partakes of the life-qualities, shows a generous heart and, if uncrossed, shows prosperity and happiness.

ii. From the Plain of Mars (or middle of the hand): This will show a life of trouble. But there is also hope and energy. There will always be struggles and obstacles but if success is achieved it will be by merit alone.

iii. From the Bracelet: This will show a fine and uncommon destiny, if found in both hands. If it goes from the Bracelet to the Mount of Saturn, ending high up on it, it shows great success (and still more certain if the line is forked). If it passes over the mount and enters the Finger of Saturn, it shows a great destiny. However, should it mount still higher and end in a star, it is said to presage a heroic career ending in violence, or a great crime!

iv. From the Mount of Luna: When the Line of Fate rises from here, it shows that all the happiness of the life will arise from the actions of some other person(s). Destiny is taken out of the hands of the subject altogether. If a Luna Line of Fate stops at the Heart Line, and there is a well-formed cross on the Mount of Jupiter, fortune and happiness will come through a good marriage.

If the line rises from below the Bracelet, it shows a very bad influence of fate and great grief.

When the Fate Line is broken, it does not necessarily mean misfortune. If the line continues again, after the break, well marked and uncrossed, it will probably indicate a great event in the life. And if the lines run parallel for a little distance, the event may bring a change for the better in position and dignity.

When chained with a double line, it is a sign of misfortune, bad character and unhappiness brought about by evil deeds.

Branches upwards from the Fate Line show improvement in position and wealth, but if they tend downwards there will be reversals and possible poverty.

In studying the Line of Fate, both hands should be carefully compared.

Line of Fortune (Solar)

This shows glory, fame and riches, artistic and literary talent; success, worldly distinction and prosperity. It should be narrow, deep, straight, long, and rise high on the Mount of Apollo. There are four places from which the line may rise:

i. From the Line of Life: This is very favorable and will show success and fortune gained by inheritance or by merit. The lower the line rises, the more surely will honor or celebrity be attained.

ii. From the Mount of Luna: In this case success or fortune will be gained unexpectedly and by the help of other people.

iii. From the Plain of Mars (middle of the hand): In this case success will come late in life, or towards middle-age, and will be the result of personal merit and exertion.

iv. From the Line of the Heart: This will show an

appreciative character, a love of art and of the beautiful; but neither wealth nor fame will be gained by it.

Cross lines are obstacles in the way of success. If they bar the line near the beginning, they will show loss of fortune by parents during youth.

A single fork on the Mount of Apollo will show success in one line of life, but if there are many forks, there will be taste and talent in many different branches of art, politics, or literature, but energy being too much distributed, nothing will be brought to success or perfection.

Unless there is a good Mount of Jupiter, a Line of Apollo cannot bring much success except in the shape of money.

The Line of Health (Hepatica)

It is a sign of a very strong constitution to be without this line. This Line of Health should start from the Bracelet, or from the Line of Life, and go on or towards the Mount of Mercury. It is very irregular and may begin or end almost anywhere in the hand. It should be long, narrow, clear, well-colored and straight. This will show good health, good memory and a kind heart. If the line is tortuous, it indicates a bad temper.

A cross on the line shows an illness, the date of which must be looked for on the Line of Life. Small lines crossing it show weakness and delicacy; often headaches and neuralgia.

The Line of Intuition (Line of Luna)

This is not a very common line and is, as a rule,

only found on imaginative or intellectual hands. It should rise on or beneath the Mount of Luna and proceed in a sort of half circle onto or towards the Mount of Mercury.

If it is clear, straight and narrow, it indicates intuition, ability to hypnotize and read others' thoughts. The subject will have a taste for the occult; for divination, clairvoyance, etc. If there is an island near the beginning of the line, there is the gift of second sight. If the line is branched, tortuous, or short, there will be danger of caprice and over-imagination, possibly even leading eventually to lunacy.

When the Line of Luna forms a triangle with the Line of Fate and the Line of the Head, it is said to indicate a good palm reader. An island on the line shows a tendency to somnambulism.

The Ring of Venus

This is a half-circle formed by a line starting from between the first and second fingers, crossing or surrounding the Mounts of Saturn and Apollo, and ending (when perfect) between the third and fourth fingers. This is generally considered a line of misfortune, since it breaks both the Line of Fate and the Line of Fortune and cuts off the Mounts of Saturn and Apollo.

THE LESSER LINES

The Plain of Mars

This is in the center of the palm of the hand; the valley through which the Line of Head flows. If it is high, it shows aggressiveness and daring. If low, the subject will never rise to any high position. The lines and signs marked on the Plain of Mars are considered under the headings of the Quadrangles and Triangles.

The Quadrangle

This is the space between the Line of Heart and the Line of Head. If it is wide and regular, largest nearest the percussion, and the lines bounding it of good color, it shows justice, loyalty and broad, tolerant views; a straightforward and courageous character. Should it be narrow it shows narrow views and conventionality; a tendency to injustice and indecision. In an otherwise good hand, but with a weak Line of Health, it often indicates asthma.

When the narrowness of the Quadrangle is caused by the Line of Head mounting towards the Line of Heart, it's a sign of irresolution and timidity.

Crosses in the quadrangle show the influences of others on the life of the subject. Those that fall downwards from the Heart Line are influences engendered by the opposite sex; those that rise up may be the result of friendship or love.

The Triangle

This is found in the center of the palm of the hand, below the Quadrangle. It's formed by the lines of Head, Life and Health. If there is no Health Line in the hand, the Line of Fortune will take its place (if that, too, is missing, then use the Fate Line).

When the Triangle is well traced, wide, and the lines are of good color, it will show good health, long life, and a strong intellect. When it is very large, it indicates audacity, generosity, and a noble character. When small and badly formed, it's a sign of meanness, avarice, and lack of intelligence.

First Angle: formed by the conjunction of the lines of Life and Head. If it is narrow, well made and acute, it will show a good disposition, sensitivity, delicacy and wit. If very obtuse, stupidity. If the lines do not actually join, great self-confidence. If the angle is formed low down, right on the Plain of Mars, it's a sign of a very unhappy life.

Second Angle: formed by the conjunction of the lines of Life and Health (or sometimes Health and Fate). If this angle is well formed it will show good health, but if it is too sharp it's a sign of a bad constitution. If it is too heavy and broad, it indicates idleness and an ill nature.

Third Angle: formed by the conjunction of the lines of Head and Health. If it is well formed and broad, it shows long life and much intelligence. If it is too sharp, a nervous temper. If badly formed, irritability often accompanied by headaches. If very obtuse, it is a sign of stupidity.

The Bracelets (Rascettes)

These are the lines which encircle the wrist. However, it's only those placed close to the hand that are important.

The Bracelets show length of life—each line being said to foretell some thirty years of existence—

also health, wealth and happiness.

A single line, well made, uncrossed and deep, shows a happy if short existence, with a calm disposition. The greater the number of lines, if equally well made, the greater the promise of good fortune and happiness.

A Bracelet of four lines is called a "Royal Bracelet," and signifies that the possessor will gain all that this world has to give.

If the lines are chained, it indicates a laborious life. If they are much broken and badly marked, it indicates trouble, distress and, with other bad signs, even disgrace.

A cross on the Bracelets is the sign of a legacy or unexpected gain. An angle promises an inheritance of some sort and an honored old age. Branches are also signs of distinction.

Lines rising from the bracelets onto the Mount of Luna show long travels. If they end in a star on the Mount, it is a warning of danger on one or more of those journeys. If the star shows up in both hands it indicates death by drowning.

The "Marriage" Lines

These are found passing horizontally across the Mount of Mercury from the percussion of the hand towards the palm.

The long lines only should be considered. They are not necessarily marriages *per se*, but great loves. Oftimes lines from the Heart Line will be found rising towards the Marriage Lines.

Stars

Stars are generally fatalities, circumstances or events over which the subject has no personal control.

Star on the Mount of Jupiter—high honor and fortune.

Star on the Mount of Saturn—danger of sudden or violent death.

Star on the Mount of Apollo—riches and unhappiness. With a good Line of Fortune, celebrity by chance and not long lasting.

Star on the Mount of Mercury—danger of theft or dishonor. In a good and talented hand it is said to be the sign of a successful author.

Star on the Mount of Mars—danger of assassination or death in battle.

Star on the Mount of Luna—danger of drowning or sign of illness.

Star on the Mount of Venus—trouble caused by love or marriage. If close to the Life Line, lawsuits.

Star on the Line of Fortune—a catastrophe.

Star on the Plain of Mars—honor and military glory.

Squares

A square is generally a good sign and gives force and energy to whichever mount or finger it may be found on. The one exception seems to be when it is found on the Mount of Venus. Then it foretells imprisonment, a convent, or other seclusion from the world.

On the lines it shows preservation from accident.

Triangles

A triangle is a favorable sign. It often indicates an aptitude for scientific pursuits.

Triangle on the Mount of Jupiter: Successful diplomacy.

Triangle on the Mount of Saturn: Love of the occult sciences, hypnotism, mysticism, superstition.

Triangle on the Mount of Apollo: Success in art or literature, scientific art, architecture, sculpture.

Triangle on the Mount of Mercury: Success in politics, or in a learned profession.

Triangle on the Mount of Mars: Military glory.

Triangle on the Mount of Luna: Reason and intuition.

Triangle on the Mount of Venus: Prudence in love, calculation in marriage.

Circles

Circles are good signs on the mounts, signifying success and glory, especially on the Mount of Apollo. But on the lines they are bad, showing misfortune. On the Line of Life, they are the sign of loss of sight.

SUMMARY

I think it can be broadly stated that the lines of the left hand show what was intended in your life; "what you were born with," as the *Rom* say. Those of the right hand show what you have made of yourself (the reverse seems to be true with left-handed people). The outline of the hand is hereditary, and it is impossible to alter it to any great degree. But the lines show the habits you encourage, the character you become.

When about to read the hands of a subject, take their left hand in your own and, holding it palm downwards, look carefully at the outline. You will then be able to judge the class of hand—long or short, pointed, spatulate, or square, with or without knots, shape of nails, etc. Then turn the hand over and press the palm so as to tell the hardness or the softness of the hand, as energy or laziness is the keynote of character and modifies all other signs. Then do the same thing with the right hand.

It is a good idea, especially when first starting, to keep a file of the hands you read. This can be done by using a fingerprint kit—the kits that are sold to enable people to take fingerprints. Rather than just inking the tips of the fingers, use a rubber roller and ink the entire hand, then press it down firmly on a sheet of clean white paper. As an alternative, sometimes a really good impression can be obtained by simply laying the hand flat on the glass plate of a Xerox, or other, duplicating machine. In this way, also, it is possible to read palms at a distance by having the client send such an impression to you through the mail. But remember to have them send you a good impression of *both hands*.

A "Reading" Style Gypsy Vardo

READING TEA LEAVES

nterpreting, or "reading," the patterns of tea leaves
eft in a cup is another very popular Romani method
of divination. It was a big favorite in the 'thirties,
forties and later, when all manner of "Gypsy Tea-
rooms" sprang up, frequently featuring very dubious
"Gypsies."

A true Romani will make a complete ritual out
of the reading, first making a pot of tea *(meski)* and
pouring a full cup for the client. Whilst the client
is drinking the tea, the Rom is carefully studying
him or her and getting initial impressions (I will talk
more about this process in "Cold Reading," below).
Some people, of course, do not like tea and do not
want to drink it. At the very least, the client should
drink three swallows of the tea. The reader can then
pour off most of the excess. Most Rom feel it is better if no milk or sugar is added—that it is "pure."

The tea most often used is Chinese tea, but
any *large-leafed* variety will do, such as Ceylon or
even mint tea (you can also read fine-leafed tea, or

even coffee grounds, but they don't seem to form
such interesting patterns). Incidentally, if you can'
get loose tea, or don't want to make a whole pot full
you can simply break open a teabag and tip the
contents into the cup, then pour in the hot water.

The cup you use should be a round one, white
or very pale colored, with a handle. However
elaborate it may be on the outside, it should have no
decoration on the inside. This should be completely
plain and with no grooves, or the like that could
influence the distribution of the tea leaves.

When the tea has been all but entirely drunk
(leave about a tablespoonful of liquid), ask the client
to take hold of the handle and rotate the cup three
times, using the left hand. Most dukkerers say that
the cup should be turned counterclockwise, but some
say that if the person is female it should be turned
counterclockwise but if male, then clockwise. As
they do this, they should swirl the liquid around the
cup, spreading the leaves around, including up
towards the rim. The client should end by tipping
the cup upside down on the saucer. I find it helps to
have a napkin on the saucer, to absorb the spilled
tea and leave you with a clean-rimmed cup for
the reading.

Finally, the client is to turn the upturned cup
around on the saucer and make a wish. In this
instance it doesn't matter in which direction it's
turned, or whether with left or right hand; it is up to
the whim of the client. Let the cup then drain for a
moment or two.

INTERPRETATION

Don't hurry the reading at all. Before saying anything, take all the time you need to look over the cup carefully and study the tea leaves. Turn the cup every way to look at the patterns from every angle. It sometimes happens that you can see two or more symbols in one cluster of tea leaves—one from one angle and another from a different angle. Always go with your first impression on a shape. You may later see another shape but don't forget that first shape.

When you begin your actual reading, start from the top of the cup and read downwards. *The handle represents the client.* Those symbols closest to the handle, therefore, will have the greatest influence on the person; those towards the far side of the cup will have only passing influence. Those on the left are generally (though not always) negative influences and those on the right, positive. Time is judged according to the positioning of the symbol, top to bottom, in the cup. At or near the upper rim is the present. The further down into the cup you go, the further into the future is the influence. So as your reading progresses, moving down, you are talking about further and further into the future. The bottom of the cup is about a year into the future. The tea leaves are not too accurate for further than that.

The way certain symbols face can also have meaning. Facing the handle (client), there is a direct effect; facing away, an indirect effect.

Don't expect all the symbols to look exactly like the things they represent. You will have to use

your imagination a great deal. You will find that there is usually just a *suggestion* of, say, a bird or a rabbit or whatever. These suggestions are enough to trigger your mind into seeing them. You'll find this especially true after a little practice. Sometimes the symbols are very distinct, yes. But more often they are not. As with so many forms of divination, the Rom use the tea leaves simply as a focal point for their own psychic powers. This is what you will be doing. In the same way, your interpretation of what you see is best coming from within you, rather than just from reading, or remembering, a long list of symbol meanings (I'll be saying this again when we discuss card reading). I will, however, give you, below, a list of the "traditional" meanings of the symbols, if only as a starting point and as examples of symbol interpretation.

Lines, straight or serpentine, generally indicate roadways, directions, a course to be taken. *Broken lines* are uncertainty or broken promises. *Circles* are completion. *Triangles*, *horseshoes*, *bells* and *crowns* frequently mean good luck. *Numbers* are important, indicating hours, days, weeks, etc., and should be given special attention.

Do notice if two or more symbols seem to tie in, one with the other(s). This is especially so where numbers appear; the number being relevant to whatever symbol it is close to.

Before listing the various symbols and their meanings, I would like to share with you an old Gypsy method for answering one of the most frequently asked questions . . . this was done to me by my grandmother and proved absolutely correct. Many young people (both male and female) want to know when they will get married. Take a teaspoon and balance it on the edge of the cup. Then carefully drip tea into the spoon, a drop at a time (not easy to do but it can be done with practice). After a number of drops, the balance will be broken and the spoon will topple into the cup. The number of drops it takes to upset it is the number of years the client has to wait before marriage.

TEA LEAF SYMBOLS
AND THEIR MEANINGS

A

ACE: The Ace of any card suit is of great significance. It indicates that powerful forces are in play. If the Ace is of the Hearts suit, it will deal with domestic and social affairs; the Diamonds suit: financial affairs; Clubs: business, especially contracts and lawsuits; Spades: sorrow, hindrances, upsets.

ACORN: Near the handle of the cup indicates coming riches; towards the far side, possible financial help through a second party.

AGE: Symbols suggesting an old man or woman indicate a breakdown in your affairs and declining fortune. All your efforts are needed just to keep going.

AIRPLANE: Swift journey. Also, a rise in life (promotion or similar) due to personal effort. A biplane suggests that the success will be due to your association with another person (in partnership or marriage).

ALLIGATOR: Great care is needed to avoid injury from others trying to harm you.

ALPS: High mountains are indicative of high ideals. Whether or not there is success will depend on what other symbols are attendant. Look also for bars or crosses nearby, or straight, clear lines. Also numbers, to get an indication of the length of time for the success to come about.

ANCHOR: Settling down and starting roots. Establishing yourself.

ANGEL: Good news on its way.

ANIMAL: See *specific animal*. Animals usually indicate action and ability to achieve in one direction or another. But each animal has its own meaning, for instance a dog for fidelity, a cat for caution, etc.

ANKLE: With foot facing away from client, shows ability misdirected, ambition without understanding, and instability of purpose. Facing client, shows soundness of judgement, deep understanding, power of direction and control.

ANT: Symbol of industry, perseverance and thrift. Success in life through your own efforts.

ANVIL: Financial gains will follow some difficulties, but it will involve quite a bit of work on your part.

ARC: Segment of a circle. Indictes an unfinished project or even career. Premature retirement; possible accident.

ARROW: Bad news to come. Probably a disagreeable letter will be received. If there are dots around it, it may be connected with money. *Note:* the direction in which it is pointing may be significant (direction from which the news will come?)

ASTERISK: There is reason for immediate attention in some direction. Check the nearby symbols. This is something that should never be overlooked.

AXE: Danger and difficulties lie ahead. Possible separation and estrangement. A loss of friends. You will be cut off from your present surroundings. Doubleheaded axe means a choice, neither possibility being good.

B

BABY: Beginning of a new enterprise. Interestingly enough Gypsies usually associate this with trouble(s); could be the start of new troubles!

BAG: This is a warning of secret enemies, plans, schemes, plots against you. The fuller the bag appears, the worse will be the condition.

BAGPIPES: Discord and disaffection in the family situation. Difficulties in business. Excitement and high tension will tend to bring on ill health and nervousness.

BALL: You will be the plaything of fortune, encountering various ups and downs over which you will seem to have no control.

BALLOON: Whether the toy balloon type or the hot air balloon, it indicates a rise in fortunes; a much needed lift.

BASKET: If seen near a house, indicates an addition to the family. It can also mean a gift, or that a legacy is coming. A basket of flowers indicates good things ahead.

BAT: False friends. Immediate need for caution. Prepare for the worst, just in case!

BEAR: Danger of running into danger through your own stupidity. You may have to overcome obstacles through sheer brute force.

BED: If the reader senses that the bed is untidy, it indicates a state of mind that will produce poor

results in the client's life and fortunes. If it seems well kept and tidy, then the fortunes will be good and life assured.

BEE: This is a really good symbol, either by itself or in combination with other symbols. It denotes prosperity as the result of industry; the acquisition of fortune; gaining wealth through trade. A general change of fortune for the good.

BELL: Much depends on what is near this symbol; basically it signifies a coming announcement. By itself, it indicates an announcement which will affect your fortunes. Near the handle it is especially fortunate. Two bells signify a marriage. Upside down, it is bad news coming.

BENCH: Stability of position. No change in circumstances, for the present.

BESOM *(Broom)*: Any possible scandal or misrepresentation will be swept away. You are in a position to clean-up your "act"; your life, your job.

BIRD: A bringer of good news. Check other symbols nearby. For example, a bird with a nest means good news concerning the home.

BOAT: A possible journey. Or a visitor expected from far away.

BOOK: An open book signifies some sort of revelation to your benfit. A closed book implies need for research, with possible trouble and expense.

BOOMERANG: Retributive justice. You are about to gather the fruits of your own actions, which may be good or bad.

BOOT: If clear and well-formed, this is a protection from danger. If rough and tattered, it indicates disgrace and loss of position.

BOTTLE: This concerns your health. You may need to check with a doctor.

BOW: This is a good sign, usually tied in with hope. It also shows the ability to grow. With an arrow it is the symbol of instant success.

BRACELET: a possible wedding or other union (could be business partnership).

BRANCH: With leaves is a sign of birth, whether children, the birth of an idea, a new venture, or whatever. Without leaves it is disappointment; barren ambitions.

BRIDE: A symbol of sorrow! Possible troubles coming.

BRIDGE: A way out of difficulties. A path over your problems.

BROOM: See *Besom.*

BUFFALO: Danger through hazardous speculation. Exercise care and forethought.

BULL: A symbol of gain and prosperity. Shows resourcefulness in business affairs and often shows that very successful financial dealings are about to take place.

BUTTERFLY: Frivolity; vanity. Advise caution. When surrounded by dots it indicates extravagance with trouble to follow.

C

CABBAGE: Usually indicates jealousy and spite. If squares are near, it can lead to disgrace.

CAGE: A symbol of marriage. If the cage is complete and clear of all other symbols, it is a marriage proposal coming.

CAKE: Pleasure; celebration. If a ring is near, it can be a wedding or anniversary approaching.

CAMEL: Progress. Often symbolizes powers of perception which can lead to a better position in life.

CANDLE: Symbol of a doer of good deeds; a philanthropist. You are likely to be of help to others and, through that, to better yourself.

CANOE: A variation on the Boat—either a visitor coming to you from far away, or *you* will be visiting someone far away.

CARRIAGE: Benefits coming from others. Your path in life will be greatly helped through close friends or acquaintances.

CART: You are about to gain in some way (probably financially) through some transaction already in hand. Trade will be plentiful and profitable. Your burdens will be light.

CASK, or **BARREL:** Empty dreams and vain ambitions. You may have to serve when you'd rather be master.

CASTLE: A prediction of high office; a good reputation and much power in your sphere of activity. You will have the favor of those in a higher office than yours.

CAT: This is the symbol of a crafty nature. Be on your guard. In business, beware of cheating and fraud. However, if the cat is in a resting position this is the symbol of domestic comfort. It is also good to have the symbol close to the handle.

CHAIR: A position of trust and affluence; satisfaction and success. It can also indicate a change of estate and a new occupation.

CHICKEN: Competence; completion; nervous energy.

CHILD: Progress and success through the use of natural powers. It is usually a very auspicious sign. Fresh enterprises and new projects will add to your prosperity.

CHIMNEY: Yours will be a position of distinction through service. You may expect changes in your environment.

CHURCH: Formality; ceremonial. Possibly some connection with birth, marriage or death. You will be associated with others of like ambition.

CIGAR: You have dreams of independence and luxury, but be careful that your best projects don't end up in smoke.

CIGARETTE: You play when you should work and indulge in trifles when there are serious matters to hand.

CIRCLE: This is the perfect form and by compliance with the natural order of things you will achieve your end and bring your work to perfection.

CLAW: Hurt and injury of a material nature by the actions of rivals and enemies. Financial loss; scandal; hurt to reputation.

CLOCK: Be attentive—"time flies and waits for no one." Be aware that time is short. This symbol can also mean (a) that there will be speedy recovery from sickness; or (b) news of a death will be forthcoming.

CLOUDS: You will be going through a dark period but have hope. You will need courage but all should turn out well.

CLOVER: Luck. If four-leafed, great luck and fortune.

CLOWN: A symbol of frivolity and inconsequence. Take yourself more seriously.

COFFIN: This does not necessarily mean death. It can be the end of a plan, a phase of life, a job, etc. It can, however, indicate failure in business or a long and serious illness.

COIN: Gain and prosperity. Financial aid.

COLUMN: Distinction and honors. You will be placed in some unique position, a position of responsibility. You will be admired.

COMET: An unexpected visitor or unexpected news.

CONE *(Pine Cone)*: Success; achievement. Fertility.

CORN: A symbol of plenty and domestic prosperity.

CORNUCOPIA: A symbol of plenty; freedom from want.

COW: A peaceful and happy existence with freedom from want. You may be called upon to make some payment; subscription; donation.

CRADLE: New projects and fresh enterprises. If the cradle is broken, it indicates trouble coming.

CROCODILE: See *Alligator*.

CROSS: Light; nucleus of energy. A source for ideas, inspiration. An opportunity will be presenting itself.

CROWN: Ascendancy over all difficulties and elevation to a high position. What you have in hand will lead to great success.

CUP: An offering. You may have to make a sacrifice, but it could lead to advancement.

D

DAFFODIL: Happiness; plans fulfilled.

DAGGER: A warning. Be on the watch for people working against you.

DAISY: Usually associated with the spring, this is a symbol of happiness and/or young love.

DEAD MAN/WOMAN: Unexpected changes of a radical nature. A dead man indicates these changes associated with a need for more alertness and intelligence; a dead woman indicates these changes associated with affections.

DEATH: This can be indicated in various ways; a skull or a black flag, for example. This is not necessarily death in the literal sense, however. It can be death of an idea, of a job, of specific plans, of a relationship . . . as such it can also indicate a new beginning and opportunities for the future. As with Dead Man/Woman (above) it means unexpected changes.

DEER: Good news from the countryside, or from a distance. Often this will entail having to make some quick decision.

DEMON/DEVIL: A sign of danger. Look out for false friends and advisers.

DICE: Possible losses through gambling.

DOG: A symbol of friendship. You can rely on the advice and assistance of close friends. If the dog is lying down, you can look forward to a period of peace and tranquility. If the dog seems to be leaping about, it is a sign of joyful news.

DOOR: Opportunity awaits.

DOT: A dot or point always emphasizes the meaning and importance of the symbol it is close to.

DRAGON: New beginnings ahead. Opportunities, but they will only come after some challenges.

DRUM: Publicity, which may not be for your own good. It can also symbolize riots and disturbances. Sometimes it indicates domestic disturbances.

DUCK: Good news.

DUMBBELL: Hard work for little profit. Rivalry and opposition.

DWARF: Disappointment and failure, with impending trouble.

E

EAGLE: a very fortunate sign indicating that aspirations will meet with tremendous success. You will attain to a much higher position than that to which you were born.

EAR: Beware of scandal.

EGG: Beneficial changes and new projects. Success probable in all things. Sometimes indicates an addition to a family.

ELEPHANT: Strength and wisdom. Success after some delay.

ENVELOPE: Unexpected news.

EQUESTRIAN: A rider on horseback indicates victory and conquest. Great success.

EXPLOSION: Impending disaster. Violent upsets and disturbances.

EYE: A symbol of intelligence. Be careful in all business dealings.

EYEGLASSES: Be extra careful in all business dealings.

F

FACE: Can be good or bad, depending on the face (take note of which way the face is looking; towards the handle or away from it). A sinister face obviously indicates troubles; a pleasant face, good things. A pleasant face that is full face (rather than profile) indicates that you will be making a discovery. More than one (pleasant) face shows new friendships.

FAN: False friends. Flirtation. Indiscretion.

FEATHER: Inconstancy; levity. Take a more serious view of your actions.

FENCE: Obstacles and limitations. Difficulties to overcome.

FENCER: Strife and arguments. Avoid litigation or your fortunes will suffer.

FILE: Disagreement and bickering.

FIR CONE/FIR TREE: Prosperity and success in inspirational types of work.

FIRE: Surprising news and hasty action. Guard your word and actions or some trouble may follow.

FISH: One of the most fortunate symbols. It shows increase and prosperity in all affairs; affluence and many profitable interests. Surrounded by dots, it means increase achieved through speculation. If wavy lines are near it, then the good fortune may fluctuate.

FIST: Guard against impulses.

FLAG: Often a danger sign, frequently associated with duty. It can also be an opportunity for service and promotion. Possibly special honors.

FLOWER(S): A single flower shows a favor granted. A bunch of flowers is a sign of many benefits and some honors. Often festivity and celebration.

FLY: Approaching annoyances. Usually connected with domestic problems. Can be an indication of scandal. When several tea leaves take the form of a swarm of flies, it indicates a number of minor annoyances.

FOOT: Understanding. You have the power of direction over your affairs. **TWO FEET:** You can move in any direction you wish.

FORK: A dilemma arising out of circumstances which you have no power to control. Many annoyances and small worries to come.

FOUNTAIN: Great success and happiness.

FOX: Be on your guard. Possible treachery.

FROG: False outlook and wrong ideas. Pride will not carry you far.

FRUIT: Always a good sign, showing increase and profit.

FUNERAL: Failure and disappointment. Look around . . . usually there are signs of change, and possibly a journey, near this symbol.

G

GALLOWS: Extreme danger of financial or social failure. Weigh every action and impulse.

GARLAND: See *flower(s)*.

GATE: If open, opportunities. If closed, a barrier or a challenge.

GHOST: Threat of danger from unexpected sources.

GIRL: Happiness, prosperity.

GLASS: Symbol of honesty but also fragility. You have nothing to regret except, perhaps, your lack of firmness.

GOAT: Misfortune through being obstinate.

GRAPES: Increase and prosperity but with accompanying burdens to be carried.

GRASSHOPPER: News coming from a distant friend.

GRAVE: News of a death.

GUARD: You have powerful friends who will stand by you.

GUITAR: Happiness in love. Pleasant surroundings.

GUN: Need for unusual care. Possibility of hurt from a distance. If a heart is nearby, this symbolizes a rival in love.

H

HALO: A halo over a figure means special honors coming to him/her.

HAMMER: Stress and strain. Persistence is called for.

HAND: Friendship, assistance, if extended towards the client (handle). Loss of opportunity, if away from client.

HANDCUFFS: Restraint, restrictions. Difficulties and frustrations.

HARE: Timidity. More than usual bravery needed. A need to be assertive.

HARP: Harmony and concord. A sign of domestic harmony and social success. In a romantic situation it indicates a happy union. If there are thick lines nearby, it shows there has been a quarrel but all will soon be reconciled.

HAT: a new occupation. Fresh projects, new ambitions

and challenges.

HATCHET: See *Axe*.

HAWK: Danger from predatory people. Be on your guard against fraud.

HEAD: See *Face*.

HEART: Happiness. Affections will be well placed. Possible engagement in marriage. Close friendship. If a crown is near, it denotes honors. If dots are near, financial gain. Two hearts together, marriage and or a very strong love affair. Look for any initials nearby.

HELMET: Protection. A position of trust.

HEN: A productive mind that will bring a position of honor, so long as you take care not to be defrauded.

HILL: The higher the hill, the better your fortunes. A symbol of attainment.

HIVE: Symbol of a home. If there is a swarm of bees it is a symbol of great success.

HORN: Glad tidings, good fortune (see also *Cornucopia*).

HORSE: Close friendships. A horse's head indicates a lover coming. A horse at full gallop is good news from someone you love dearly.

HORSESHOE: Universal symbol of good luck, usually brought about by apparent chance.

HOURGLASS: You must act quickly, time is running out. Be watchful over those near and dear to you.

HOUSE: Safety, possession. A contented life.

I

INSECT: Troubles and vexations. Small irritations.

IVY: A sign of loyal friends.

J

JAVELIN: See *Spear*

JESTER: See *Clown*

JUG: A symbol of influential friendships and general well-being. You will be of use to others and, in so doing, benefit yourself. You will have a lot of good friends.

K

KANGAROO: Unexpected travel plans.

KETTLE: Domestic happiness.

KEY: There are important decisions to be made. You may be entering upon a new path. Carefully consider all new proposals made to you at this time. If you use your opportunities with intelligence, you could unlock the doors to great prosperity and happiness.

KITE: Unusual ambitions. It is within your power to reach to great heights. If the kite is without a tail, however, it is the sign of vain ambitions and projects that may end badly.

KNIFE: Beware of people out to harm you. With the blade pointed towards the handle, it indicates false friends. With the hilt towards the handle, it indicates that you are in command but need to take precautions and be alert. Crossed knives indicate arguments.

L

LADDER: Opportunities for advancement. If dots are near, opportunities for making money.

LAMB: Changes coming about. New ideas, innovations coming into being.

LAMP: Things previously hidden will be revealed. Lost property will be recovered.

LANTERN: See *Lamp*

LEAF: News, letters, messages. Many leaves signify good news, happiness and success.

LEG: This is a sign of strength and fortitude, also of progress. Note the direction in which the leg is facing.

LETTER: As might be assumed, a letter means news is coming, though it could be good or bad. Look for other symbols nearby. For example, a letter with a heart nearby would mean a love letter, or news from a loved one; with a dollar sign nearby would mean financial news, etc.

A letter of the alphabet is an initial for someone's name. Again, see what other symbols are nearby.

LIGHTHOUSE: Exercise caution, there is trouble ahead.

LINES: Lines show direction, journeys, progress. The most favorable lines are straight and unbroken. Double lines are roads. Broken lines are uncertainty and broken promises.

LION: Supremacy. Your position will improve. Your leadership will be recognized.

LOAF OF BREAD: Your "daily bread." Much depends on what is near. It could mean happiness, increase, well-being or it could mean unhappiness, sickness, loss.

LOCK: An obstacle to your progress. A difficult problem that needs to be solved.

M

MAN: A visitor. If the figure is facing the handle, the

visitor will be staying for a period. If facing away from the handle, he will only be there briefly.

MEDAL: A sign of distinction and honor. An award for work done. Success in an undertaking, with recognition of that success.

MERMAID: Strength will be needed to resist temptation.

MONK: A symbol for deception and subterfuge. Be very cautious. Some unpleasant incident connected with a man of position or influence will tend to hurt your prospects.

MONKEY: Danger from flattery. Be on your guard.

MOON: Possible romantic attachment. New ideas. Start of new undertakings.

MOUNTAINS: Great ambitions together with challenges. You will attain great heights, but not without much effort.

MOUSE: Poverty. Neglected opportunities. Possibility of burglary.

MUSHROOM: Advancement through expansion and growth. Can also mean danger to a house in the country.

N

NAIL: This symbol denotes malice and cruelty which may be directed against you. Your feelings are going to be hurt.

NECKLACE: If complete, a conquest and many admirers. If broken, danger of losing the love of one you adore.

NUMBER/NUMERAL: Any number has significance for the symbol(s) it is near. It could be symbolizing time—hours, days, weeks, etc.—or it could be indicating an amount, as with money, or the days of the week themselves. Numbers in themselves do have significance, however. Briefly they are as follows:

One—The number of the Sun. Happiness, success, dignity and honors.

Two—The number of the Moon. Relativity. The dualism of life. The relationship of opposites.

Three—Mars. The three parts of time: past, present and future. If badly placed, can mean accident, fire, quarrels. If in the clear, resolution.

Four—Mercury. The number of reality and concretion.

Five—Jupiter. Joy, good fortune, good harvest. Increase and propogation.

Six—Venus. The number of cooperation. Harmony, peace, satisfaction. Also pleasures and entertainment.

Seven—Saturn. The number of completion. It indicates wisdom, balance, rest and perfection.

Eight—Uranus. Dissolution, separation. In the clear it denotes inspiration, genius and invention.

Nine—Neptune. Can be exile but also pertains to spiritual perception.

NURSE: Illness, though not necessarily the client's.

O

OVAL: See *Egg*

OWL: A sinister omen. If the client is about to go into a new venture, s/he will probably fail. Indicative of trouble and loss in business unless great precaution is taken.

OX: A sign of prosperity and the friendship of persons in high position.

P

PAGODA: A sign of traveling in distinguished company.

PALM TREE: After a career of hard work you will be in a position to retire to the home of your choice. You only have to take advantage of opportunities presented in order to succeed.

PARACHUTE: You will escape from some great danger. You aim high and run the risk of falling, but you will always land on your feet.

PEACOCK: Luxury; splendor; elegance. A life of luxury. If there is a ring nearby it denotes a wealthy marriage.

PIG: Good luck. You will not want for food. However, there is a danger of excess through self-indulgence.

PILLAR: A symbol of strength and support.

PILLORY: See *Stocks*

PIPE: Take time to contemplate and review your position in life. A break, for replanning and re-grouping, is necessary.

PISTOL: Danger. Possible disaster. Exercise caution. (also see *Gun*)

PONY: See *Horse*

PUMPKIN: The symbol for a warmhearted person; someone with a good nature. A diplomat, capable of appealing to others' finer feelings.

PUPPY: A frivolous and insincere nature. Inability to focus on any one thing at a time. Indecision.

PYRAMID: This symbolizes a great secret that will be revealed. This may be a secret that has held you back in some way. Its revelation will enable you to move forward rapidly. It is, basically, a sign of coming good fortune.

Q

QUIVER: A quiver of arrows symbolizes power of command. The ability to lead. You have a message to deliver and will deliver it, come what may.

QUESTION MARK: The unknown. There will be frustrations and many questions that will be unanswered. You need to search for those answers.

R

RABBIT: A sign of timidity. A need to be more assertive. You hesitate too much before making decisions.

RACQUET: (as used in tennis, racquetball, etc.) A contest to come. Possibility of trouble and arguments. If the handle of the racquet is towards the cup handle, you will come out on top. If away from it, you will lose.

RAINBOW: A sign of hope and encouragement.

RAKE: A careful and industrious nature. A tendency to pay attention to the small details.

RAT: Losses through enemies. Be cautious.

RAVEN, ROOK or CROW: You have a roving nature. Your life tends to be shiftless and could easily include illegal activities. You tend to horde things—of your own and of other peoples!

REVOLVER: See *Gun*

RING: This is always a sign of goodwill and friendship which can lead to important events in your life. It can, and often does, tie in with marriage—look for other symbols, and especially initials, nearby. It can also symbolize the completion of a project.

ROSE: See *Flower*. The rose can, also, have a connection with a possible marriage.

S

SADDLE: You possess the faculties that will equip you for traveling and exploration. You will soon be sent on a journey.

SAW: Hard work.

SCAFFOLD: The possibility of a law action against you. You will need the best defense you can find.

SCALES: Judgement at hand. If the scales are tipped, note which way they go. If they are "heavy" towards the cup handle, judgement will be in your favor.

SCISSORS: Misunderstandings; confusion; people working at cross-purposes. Possible separation.

SCORPION: A sign of danger. Be very careful, especially in your business dealings.

SHARK: Someone of a predatory nature. Note its proximity to the handle.

SHEEP: See *Lamb*

SHIP: Success. Good fortune. Your efforts are finally being justly rewarded.

SHOE: A messenger is on his way, with good news.

SKELETON: Possibility of sickness and want. Lean times are coming. You will have to depend on the friendship of others.

SKULL: Danger. Be very careful in all dealings with

other people.

SLEIGH: Rapid progress. Little opposition to your plans.

SNAKE: Danger from an enemy. Be especially cautious in business. If the snake has its head away from the handle, then you will be the eventual winner.

SOLDIER: Fighting, arguments, opposition.

SPADE: Steady work ahead. Work hard and you will be justly rewarded.

SPEAR: Wounding, either physically or from scandal.

SPIDER: Cunning, possible ensnarement. If you use cunning and caution, you can become very rich.

SPIRAL: Your progress will seem slow and tedious but you are slowly but surely working your way to the top.

SPOON: An energetic nature, forever striving. You are not afraid to "stir things up" if you think it will help your cause.

SQUARE: Limitation. Sometimes of sinister meaning. Be cautious.

STAR: Good fortune. Opportunities for advancement. A special occasion about to be announced.

STEEPLE: High aspirations. Ambition.

STOCKS or PILLORY: Restraint. Frustration through being unable to take action.

SUBMARINE: Hidden enemies. Proceed with especial caution.

SUN: Fortune. Great happiness. Success.

SWAN: A lover. Good luck in love. Notice if there is an initial nearby.

SWORD: A menace or a protection—notice which way it is pointing. Pointing towards the handle, it is a threat or menace. Pointing away, it is protection.

T

TABLE: You are going to be called to a reunion of some sort. A gathering of friends.

TEAPOT: Consultations; committee meetings.

TENTS: Danger of coming troubles. A warning to be on your guard.

TORCH: The symbol for a progressive and pioneer type of character. It denotes a calling; a leader in some movement.

TORTOISE or TURTLE: Slow advancement with much hard work. Little to show for your efforts immediately, though you will reap the reward eventually.

TRAIN: Change. Possible travel.

TREE: A wish will be fulfilled. An oak tree denotes protection and security.

TRIANGLE: Always a good sign. Good luck; success in new enterprises.

TRIDENT: Authority. Possible promotion. A position of respect.

U

UMBRELLA: If open, protection from trouble. If closed, frustration in seeking protection.

V

VASE: a sign of service, by you, to friends.

VIOLIN: a reclusive and independent person. Someone who spends much of their time in study and contemplation. Very much the individualist.

VOLCANO: A passionate person, frequently with an explosive temper. Violence; sudden passion.

VULTURE: Cruelty and oppression. Possibility of theft.

W

WALKING STICK or CANE: A friend will be visiting you.

WEB: Listen to the advise of friends or you could get tangled up in a situation that would be difficult to get out of.

WHALE: You are about to undertake a considerable piece of work which will eventually reward you well, though not for two to three years.

WHEEL: Progress. Also indicates a need for patience, insofar as "if you wait long enough the wheel will eventually turn full circle."

WIG: A sign of deception and false information.

WINDMILL: Grandiose plans will bring big rewards.

WINGS: News coming. Could be good or bad.

WISHBONE: An inheritance.

WITCH: Wisdom; sage advice.

WOLF: Intrigue. Great cleverness.

WOMAN: A visitor bearing good news. Look for other symbols nearby for an indication of the type of news.

Y

YACHT: See *Ship*.

YOKE: A position of submission; of service. Hard

work for someone else.

Z

ZEBRA: Special distinction. You are sought out as a friend.

ZODIAC: You will often see the symbols for the signs of the zodiac. You can read them according to the interpretations given in the many books on astrology; the effect on the subject being construed by the nearness of the sign to the cup handle. In addition (or as an alternate way of reading them) you can use the very quick overview of the signs' meanings as follows:

Aries—Impulsive changes; excitement. Progess.

Taurus—A sign of money, wealth.

Gemini—A letter. Possibly a short journey.

Cancer—The home. If a ship or arrow is near, it indicates a long journey.

Leo—Pleasures. Children. Sports.

Virgo—Domestic affairs. The accessories of daily life.

Libra—Libra— Marriage. Contracts.

Scorpio—Loss. Personal danger. Secret enemies.

Sagittarius—Long voyages. Messages from abroad.

Capricorn—Realization of ambitions. Wishes granted.

Aquarius—Friendship. Social gathering.

Pisces—Restraint. Voluntary seclusion. Confinement.

For any other symbols that you may see, which

I have not listed here, simply use your intuition.
Indeed, if your intuition tells you, strongly, something different from what I have listed above, *go
with that intuition*. As with all divination, the symbols seen and used are simply focal points for your
own psychic feelings.

CRYSTAL GAZING

A popular conception of the Gypsy fortuneteller is one of a figure sitting at a table and gazing into a crystal ball. The truth is that although many Gypsies (especially the *Shuvanis)* can see things in the crystal, they cannot necessarily do so on demand; at the whim of the fee-paying client. This is one facet of divination that does call for a certain amount of preparation (both physical and mental) and cannot be done on a round-the-clock basis. For this reason, many Romani *dukkerers* don't even bother to do it properly most of the time. They simply sit with the ball in front of them, and then go by their own intuition in reading the client. Or as a last resort, if nothing seems to be coming to them, do what is known as a "cold reading" (I will be talking about cold readings at the end of the book).

The majority of people do have the ability to see into a crystal ball. As with so many things, it's simply a question of practice. To start, you should work in a room where you will be undisturbed and that is perfectly quiet. You do not want to be distracted in any way, initially, so make sure you are alone and that no one is going to come into the room unexpectedly. Sit in a good, straight-backed chair that is comfortable. Have the crystal ball on a table at a comfortable height in front of you.

Any good reflective surface will do for your gazing: a crystal, a magnifying lens, a highly polished dark-colored surface, a glass of water . . . yes, a glass of water! Take a regular tumbler (*clear* glass, not decorated) and fill it almost to the brim with water. It will work well. Whatever you use, stand it on a black background, such as a piece of black velvet. This is so that as you gaze at the object you will not be distracted by anything around it.

Initially, you should have very little light in the room. Later you will be able to do this anywhere, but to start with try to have everything in your favor. I would suggest just a single candle, which should be placed behind you so that you do not see it directly reflected in the crystal. I would further suggest that you burn some incense. I do find that this helps; inducing the right feelings, the right atmosphere. It does actually affect the vibrations of the area. Any good, pleasant-smelling incense will do (*e.g.* frankincense or sandalwood). Gypsies burn a lot of incense. It certainly does seem to give a very special "atmosphere" to the room where the reading is taking place.

Now the only secret—if there is a secret—to crystal gazing is in learning to "gaze." *Don't stare!* Don't try to look into the crystal, never once blinking your eyes. All you'll get is eye strain! No. Just relax.

Look into the crystal. When you need to blink, just blink (try not to even think about whether or not you are blinking or you'll probably get hung up on it and be concentrating more on blinking, or not blinking, than on anything else! Just relax).

Breathe deeply; inhaling fully and then exhaling fully. Don't try to picture/imagine anything in the crystal. Just look into it. For the first several times you do this, you will probably experience nothing but disappointment. You may try for a week or two, or three, with no results. But don't give up. Suddenly it will happen. Don't keep up the gazing for too long at any one session. I would recommend you do not try for longer than ten—absolute maximum, fifteen—minutes at any one time. If nothing has happened, just put away your crystal and try again the next night. Incidentally, *some* people do get results right away, first time out.

But what will finally happen is that you will see a picture in the crystal. Now you may have a little preliminary "display" just before this. Most people do. You may get the feeling that the crystal is some-how slowly filling with smoke, or clouds (usually white in color). As you gaze into it, you will see the whole ball (or water glass, or whatever) filling with swirling white clouds. Then, almost immediately, the clouds will start to fade away again. As they disperse you will be left with a picture, just like looking into a small three-dimensional television set. This picture may be either in black-and-white or in full color, though most people seem to see in color. Also, it may be a moving picture or it may be a still, like a

regular photograph. Again, most people see moving images.

What you actually see is frequently symbolic—which would tend to give support to the theory that what you see is actually coming from inside you, rather than from any outside source. Interpreting it can be a problem. To give an example: You might see a picture of a squirrel running up a tree and pausing at a fork in the branches before running on up one of the limbs. What does that mean, you wonder? What has that to do with anything? On reflection, it should become obvious. It indicates that the person for whom you are reading will shortly have to face a decision, and that decision will affect the direction of his or her life in the immediate future.

Not everything will be presented in these veiled terms, of course, but do be prepared. Many times first-time crystal gazers say, "I saw all sorts of things but none of it made the slightest bit of sense!" Well, it does make sense if you just take the time to interpret. It's interesting to compare what is seen in a crystal to what is seen in dreams. There is a great similarity between dream interpretation and the interpretation of crystal images.

When starting, you pretty much have to accept just whatever is presented to you, indiscriminately. You can, however, learn to see just what you want to see—most important when doing a reading, on request, for someone else. All you do is meditate for a brief moment before starting to gaze. Meditate on what it is that you want to see; the question that you want answered or the information you need to obtain. This meditation need only take a moment or two, just enough time to deliver the message to your unconscious mind. Then, clear your (conscious) mind of all thoughts, breathe deeply, and gaze into the crystal *now trying to keep your mind blank.* Shortly the crystal will cloud (though not always), then clear and present the thing you wanted to see. It's as simple as that.

Even when you are getting good information, with images flowing freely and delivering all that you want, don't keep at it for too long. Limit yourself to, say, a half hour maximum from the time you start to see things. You can always come back later and pick up from where you left off. I would suggest a fifteen minute break between sessions. And as I said above, when first trying and being unsuccessful, limit yourself to just ten minutes or so. There is a far greater strain when first getting started.

As you progress and become more practiced and accomplished at crystal gazing, you will be able to change the circumstances in which you do it. You will eventually be able to do your work in full daylight (though some sort of low light *is* best, as with watching television) and with someone sitting opposite you asking questions. Initially, however, try to eliminate all distractions.

A final word on the crystal itself, if you are opting to use the real thing. What size should it be? The answer is, whatever is most comfortable for you. The problem with using over-large balls is that they invariably have imperfections in them which tend to distract the beginner. My favorite size is about

Quartz Crystal Ball
Photo by Frank Dorland

three to four inches in diameter. I prefer to have the ball on a stand, but you may prefer to hold it in the palm of your hand; many people do.

The ball does not have to be of pure lead crystal (as should be obvious from the fact that you can actually gaze into virtually any reflective surface). An amethyst ball can be wonderful, as can rose quartz, obsidian, or any other variety. Quartz, glass, or even a plastic ball can be used. With a glass crystal ball, avoid any with bubbles in them, at least to start with. Try to get a ball with as few imperfections as possible; best with no imperfections whatsoever. Here one of the acrylic plastic balls may be best initially. The only real problem with these is that they scratch very easily, so great care must be taken in their handling.

Once you are accomplished at the art, then you'll find that imperfections in the ball don't worry you at all. But, as I said above, when starting out you might as well have everything going for you that you can. In fact, if only from that standpoint, I favor a quartz crystal rather than glass or plastic, for a true crystal ball does more than just act as a viewfinder for you. It builds up an energy field around you. It actually emits vibrations, setting up a whole ambience, an atmosphere conducive to scrying, complementing that put out by the incense burning. As I mention in the chapter on Crystals and Gemstones, a future book of mine will deal with the properties and uses of crystals and stones, as used by the Romanies, and the energy fields that they produce.

Most Rom simply regard their crystal balls as

tools. Yet the tools of any worker who cares are treated with respect. So with the crystal ball. Keep it wrapped in a piece of black silk when not in use. When you first get it, and then again at every Full Moon, wash it carefully in clear water, dry it, and then expose it to the direct light of the Moon for a half-hour or more. By direct light I mean not moon-light coming through a window pane . . . open the window and let the actual rays fall on the crystal. Never expose the crystal to direct sunlight.

The Gypsy Quadrilles c. 1969

CARD READING

As I've mentioned before, when having their fortunes told people love to see objects being used. Frequently they attribute almost "magickal" properties to these objects. They stare fixedly into the crystal ball, along with the seer, hoping to catch a glimpse of all that is there. They lock their gaze onto their own palm as though they had never seen it before, and look desperately for indications of those things they are being told. But especially they love to study the cards, even if they have no idea whatsoever of their interpretation. Tarot cards are popular, not just because of the mystique that has built up around them, but also because most decks have a different picture on each card and therefore go further than most other forms of divination in giving the unknowledgeable querent some kind of clue as to why the seer says what he or she does.

The tarot cards came from India, as did the Gypsies themselves. In India today there is found a deck of fortunetelling cards called the *atouts*, in many respects similar to the tarot. The earliest known tarot decks date from approximately the same time that the Gypsies started leaving India and spreading across Europe. It would seem to follow, then, that we have the Gypsies to thank for giving us these wonderful divinatory cards. Yet many dukkerers are just as happy using regular playing cards as they are using the tarot. I don't think there is any significance to this. Playing cards developed from the tarot anyway, with the suit of cups becoming hearts, pentacles becoming diamonds, wands becoming clubs and swords becoming spades. In this section, then, I will look at the use of both tarot cards and ordinary playing cards.

Tarot Cards

Today there are over two hundred fifty different decks of tarot cards on the market. Which of these you choose to use is your preference. The Rom don't seem to have any general consensus on this. I have seen many; most of them handed on down through the Gypsy family. Some of them are even made by the Gypsies themselves, based on the traditional designs. My personal favorites are the Morgan-Greer deck, the Hanson-Roberts deck, the Crowley Thoth deck and a Royal Fez Moroccan deck that I have colored myself, to give it my own *mana*. I am also presently hand-making a deck of my own,* based on some of the original Gypsy designs I have

---

* *Buckland's Gypsy Fortunetelling Deck* is available through Llewellyn Publications. Please write for catalog.

een. So, it's up to you. I suggest you try several and
ee which one you most enjoy working with.

Significator and Cards

The method of working is for the client to
hoose a certain number of the cards and for the
reader to lay out those cards in a special order, each
position being given a particular meaning. The reader
hen interprets them, reading both from the individual
ard and from its position and its relationship to the
other cards.

Usually one card is chosen, at the outset, to
epresent the querent in the reading (Significator).
The favored Romani method of choosing this is for
he reader to go through *all* the cards in the deck and
o pick out one card that she feels is most representa-
ive of her client. This she determines simply from
"feelings." If you happen to know, very well, the per-
on for whom you are reading then it is usually
airly easy to find a card that seems to be just right.
But if you are reading for a stranger, you certainly
need to somehow "tune-in" and then connect up
with one particular card.

The Gypsy way of "tuning in" is through psychometry. "Cross my palm with silver" is a familiar
Gypsy greeting before fortunetelling. Yet this is not
just a way to get payment for the reading. When the
client passes across the "piece of silver" (or dollar
bill, or whatever), he is giving the reader something
which he has handled; something which will make a
connection between the two of them. From this the
Gypsy can then determine—usually with amazing
accuracy—which of the seventy-two tarot cards is the

right one to use to represent that person. You may not be proficient at psychometry (it's actually just a question of practice. See my *Buckland's Complete Book of Witchcraft*, Lesson Eight), but you can soon become extremely accurate at picking out the right card. I suggest you start by actually holding the client's hands in yours. Take his hands, close your eyes, and meditate for a moment on the person. Keep your mind open and try to get a feeling for the type of person he is. Is he happy or unhappy? Carefree or worried? Short-tempered or easygoing? Try to picture him in a home environment, then in a working one. Whether or not you get clear pictures, don't worry too much about it. Release the hands and pick up the cards. Go fairly quickly through the deck until you come to one card that seems to say to you "Hey! This is him!" And there *will* be one. If you can't find it, go quickly through all the cards a second time.

When I do this, I go through till I find the one card, *but then I keep on going*. Usually I get to the end of the deck and am certain that the one I picked was right. But sometimes, as I continue, I find one or two more that seem equally suitable! If so, then I place the two or three cards together in a line and once again take my client's hands. Just holding the hands and looking at the now-narrowed choice I find directs me to one particular card much more strongly than the others.

But supposing, no matter how hard you try, you just can't get any feeling; just can't find the "right" card to represent your client? Then (as a last resort) give the deck to him and ask *him* to pick out the one which he feels is most representative of himself.

Many books on the tarot state that you have very few choices for the querent's card. They say that if, for example your client is an older, dark-haired woman then you should use the Queen of Swords as her card . . . nonsense! Everyone is an individual, and so everyone will be represented by a different card.

Once you have selected the client's card, put it to one side and give him the rest of the deck to shuffle. As he shuffles them, ask him to concentrate his thoughts on any questions or problems he may have. Then he must cut the cards, with his left hand, into three piles. You turn over those three piles and study, and read, the top cards. You read them as individual cards first, then in combination. This is known as a General Reading and will give some sort of an idea as to how the main reading is going to go, particularly as it applies to the question the client was concentrating upon.

You next stack up the cards again and then spread them, face down, across the table and ask him to pick out ten of them (the number he is to pick will actually depend upon the layout you are going to use—see below). These he must place in a pile, one on top of the others, face down, in the order in which he draws them. These chosen cards, together with the one already drawn as his Significator, are the ones that will be used in the reading. The others may be put to one side.

When laying out the chosen cards, they are

always laid face down (with the exception of the Significator, which is kept face up). They should also be laid down *in the order in which they were chosen*—the first card chosen should be laid down first, the second laid second, and so on. Since the first card the client chose is at the bottom of the pile, you can simply lay them down dealing off the bottom. But here is a way I have found more convenient—at least for me. The cards, as chosen by the client, are in their pile with the first one picked on the bottom and the others piled on top, as described above. In other words, in reverse order to the way you want to use them.

Simply take up the pile and count them out, placing the top card on the table, the next one on top of it, the next on that, and so on. What you are doing, then, is reversing the order to bring the first chosen card to the top of the pile. And you are also doing this—counting them out—for the useful purpose of ensuring that the correct number of cards had been picked. Working from there, you can then deal off the top of the pile, laying down that first chosen card in the first position, and so on.

Let's look at layouts first. I will deal with actual interpretation of the cards afterwards.

LAYOUTS

No one layout seems more popular than others with the Gypsies. They use whatever they have found to work best for them. As with the cards themselves, many use layouts that have been passed down through the family and may not be found anywhere else. Here are a few that I have found in use.

1: *The Star*

For this layout the client chooses *twenty-four* cards. They are laid out around the Significator, in the form of a star. Going in a *counterclockwise* direction, lay the first eight cards face down and equally spaced around the center Significator. Start in the top center position and finish at the top right. Then lay the next eight on top of these and the final eight on top of those.

Start the reading by turning over the first set of three cards (top center). Proceed again in a counterclockwise direction.

Reading from this layout, the positions of the cards do not carry any specific meaning. The cards are read almost like a narrative, a story; going straight on from one pile to the next around the Significator.

2. *The Fan*

Thirteen cards are drawn for this layout. They are spread, face down, in the shape of a fan above the Significator. The cards are read in groups of five, the fifth card becoming the first card of the next group each time. This gives three groupings. The first group represents the *past*. The second group, the *present*. And the third group, the *future*. The middle (third) card of each group is then drawn out and they are placed together. They are now read in relation to one another to give a general reading or summary.

The Star

3. *The Council*

[It is of passing interest, perhaps, that this spread involves thirteen cards—the number traditionally found in a Wiccan coven—and is called "The Council" . . . of Elders?]

Twelve cards are picked by the client. The Significator is placed, face up, in the center of the table. The twelve are laid down as follows:

The first card is placed to the right of the Significator, the second to the left. The third goes above it and the fourth below. Number five goes to the far right (beside number one) and six to the far left (beside two). Similarly, seven goes to the top (above three) and eight to the bottom (below four). Nine goes to the top right (beside three) and ten top left (on the other side of three). Eleven goes bottom right (to the right of four) and twelve bottom left (left of four).

Once again there are no specific meanings for the positions, but the *groupings* of the cards for interpretation is very interesting. Number seven, at the top, is considered first. Then the full horizontal line below it: Ten, Three and Nine. Then Six, followed by the full vertical line of Ten, Two and Twelve. Next the vertical line of Nine, One and Eleven, followed by Five. Then the horizontal line of Twelve, Four and Eleven. And, finally, Eight. All of these are read according to their proximity to the Significator.

It may sound somewhat complicated, but reference to the diagram will show that it is actually fairly straightforward.

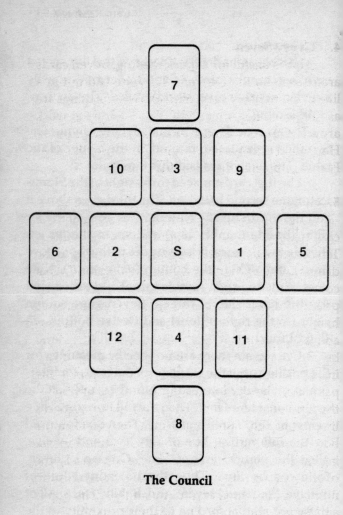

The Council

4. *Gypsy Seven*

This is useful for a quick reading. Seven cards are chosen by the Querent. They are laid out in a line to the right of the Significator. The meanings are as follows: One—Inner Self. Two—Forces at work around Querent. Three—Past influences. Four—Hopes and Dreams. Five—Family and Friends. Six—Forces opposing. Seven—Final Outcome.

5. *Keltic Cross*

This is probably the most popular layout in tarot card reading and is used by quite a number of *Rom*. Ten cards are picked and are laid out according to the diagram. The first is covering the Significator ("What covers him"—*i.e.* the outward appearance that he presents). The second crosses the first ("What crosses him"—*i.e.* forces working aginst him). The third goes above ("What crowns him"—his ideals), and the fourth below ("Beneath him"—the real him, deep down inside). The fifth goes to the right ("Behind him"—the past), and the sixth to the left ("In front of him"— the immediate future). The remaining four go in a line to the right of this cross, being placed from the bottom up to the top: seventh—"His house," meaning his close friends and family; eighth—"Himself," the overall person (often a synthesis of the Significator, numbers one, three and four); ninth—"His hopes and fears;" and ten—"The final outcome."

6. *Buckland Seven Star*

This is a layout that my grandmother would use a lot. Although I have never found it anywhere

Keltic Cross

else, I am including it here both for her sake and because I think it's a very good layout! It uses only the twenty-two Major Arcana cards and is used for examining the immediate future . . . the next six to twelve months at the most.

The Fool is always used to represent the client, as the Significator, in this layout. My grandmother never referred to it as "The Fool," however, but as "The Seeker," and she always seemed able to relate the card to the individual in some way.

The Significator is laid in the middle of the table, and the other twenty-one cards are well shuffled by the client. They are then laid down around this center, three at a time, in the form of an upturned seven-pointed star. Start laying them down in the top right-hand corner and proceed clockwise.

The cards are read in their threes. The meaning of the positions is as follows:

1: *Events* (affecting the client) *presently coming to an end*. In other words, a brief look at what has gone before and is just finishing up.

2: *Events beginning to come together*. What is shaping up for the immediate future.

3. *Hopes and Fears* (of the client).

4. *Inner Strength*. What the client is able to draw upon, from her/himself, to handle the forces which affect her or him.

5. *Positive energies available*. This represents the energies that can be called upon if needed; those of close friends, situations, events, etc. Sometimes those actual people and events can be read in these cards.

Final Outcome — 19, 20, 21

Events Ending — 1, 2, 3

Negative Energies — 16, 17, 18

S

Events Beginning — 4, 5, 6

Positive Energies — 13, 14, 15

Hopes and Fears — 7, 8, 9

Inner Strength — 10, 11, 12

Buckland Seven Star

6. *Negative energies* that may be drawn in. Again from other people, situations, events, etc.

7. *Final Outcome.* The overall result of the forces at work in this time period. *Note:* this is the final outcome of this particular set of forces, not of the client's life in general.

These are probably the most popular layouts that I have found amongst the Gypsies. Others are used, of course. In fact many of the layouts that I give below for the use of regular playing cards can be used just as effectively for tarot cards, and *vice versa*.

INTERPRETATION

Now that I have dealt with the layouts, let's look at the actual interpretation of the cards. For this I think I can probably do no better than repeat what I said in my book *Buckland's Complete Book of Witchcraft*:

"How, then, do you interpret? Go by your instincts; your feelings, your intuition. As you turn over each card, think of the position that it occupies. For example (in the Keltic Cross layout): position #6–the Immediate Future. What, of the illustration on the card, strikes you most forcibly as you turn it face up? Invariably one thing— one small part of the overall design—will "hit your eye" first. Think of what that object, color or symbol, can mean in relation to (in this example) the Querant's immediate future. For example, suppose you are using a Rider-Waite deck . . . and you turn up the "Death" card. Does this mean Death is in the near future? No! The interpretation given in one book is, "transformation; change. Sometimes followed by or preceding destruction. Sometimes birth or renewal." It could mean the death of an idea, or a job—perhaps leading to "rebirth" in a new job (incidentally, I should mention here that it will help immeasurably if you *disregard the titles* on the Major Arcana cards. "Death" is not necessarily death; "Justice" is not necessarily justice; the "Devil" not necessarily the Devil, and so on).

"By going by our method, there are far more possibilities. You might be struck by the small boat in the background and associate it with travel. Or you might be impressed by the sun rising (or setting?) between the two towers on the right; or the rose on the banner; or the bishop-like figure . . . there are so many things which might strike you forcibly. You will find it a different thing each time you read the cards, giving a different—and therefore far more personal—reading for each individual. So, don't go by (any book of interpretation) . . . use your own powers."

I would just add to that, that what you see should be told to the client in as easy a narrative style as possible. You don't have to say *why* you say what you say (unless you are specifically asked). And there's no need to mix your words with mystical, esoteric terms to try to impress and make it sound more profound! If you do see "bad news"— possible death or an accident—then choose your words especially carefully. Suggest that the client take special precautions, or try to avoid certain undertakings. After all, don't forget that what you are seeing is only an indication of what is *likely* to happen if things proceed as they are. But *NOTHING*

HAS TO BE. Anything can be changed, for we do create our own reality.

I have mentioned the four suits of the tarot: Wands, Cups, Pentacles and Swords. In your interpreting the cards, remember that Wands are frequently associated with sexual pursuits and feelings, also with projects and undertakings. Cups are associated with love and close friendships. Pentacles are often indicative of money, and Swords of troubles and misfortunes.

One last word . . . at the very beginning, the client concentrated on a particular question when first shuffling the cards. That question should have been answered in the course of the reading. When you finish, *ask* if it was answered. If he says "No," then ask what the question was, and look back over the cards. The answer will be there. It usually comes out naturally, as part of the reading, but sometimes it doesn't so you have to look more specifically.

Playing Cards

As I said above, many Rom dukkerers are quite happy to use regular playing cards rather than tarot cards. I think this is because they are able to draw on their psychic powers a lot more easily, perhaps, than other people are. They are therefore able to "read" from the plain *pips* on the cards without having to rely on actual pictures presented for interpretation. Of course it isn't hard for anyone to learn the meanings of fifty-two different cards though, as with the tarot, there is a lot more to a good reading than just repeating book-learned equivalents.

As with the start of a tarot reading, as the client shuffles the cards, he (or she) should concentrate on any question, or problem, that he is particularly concerned about. And, again, that question should be answered during the course of the reading.

After the shuffling you may (if you like—this is not mandatory) have the client cut them into three piles, so that you can turn them over and give a quick general reading from the top three cards.

If you are doing a reading using only a certain number of cards, then spread the deck, face down, across the table and let him pick that number (as in the tarot instructions above). If you are using all the cards, simply stack them up and start working with them.

Significator

A card to represent the Querent is not always used when reading from playing cards. When one is used, however, it is one of the court cards: for a man, one of the Kings; for a woman, one of the Queens. For a very young person—male or female—use the Jacks. The particular suit chosen depends upon the client's coloring: white skin = Diamonds; medium fair skin = Hearts; medium dark skin = Clubs; dark skin = Spades.

LAYOUTS

As will be seen, some of thse layouts use the complete deck. Others use a modified deck of thirty-two cards: that is, a deck with only the aces, kings, queens, jacks, tens, nines, eights and sevens. Everything below the sevens is dropped out.

1. *The Pyramid*

The client, after thoroughly shuffling the whole deck, will hand the cards to you. You will lay down the Significator, face up, as the top card of the pyramid. Beneath it, from the deck, lay the next two cards. Beneath them lay the next three cards. Beneath them the next four, and so on. Continue putting down cards until you have seven rows.

The top row (the solitary Significator) of course represents the client. The second row represents the influences presently strongest around him. The third row is the powers he can draw upon—friends, influence, etc. The fourth row are those forces working against him. The fifth row shows his past. The sixth shows his hopes, fears and dreams. And the seventh row indicates the final outcome.

Comment on any pairs, triplets, or quartettes (two, three or four of a kind that happen to lay side by side, see below in *Interpretation*).

Now study the last card laid down in each row (including the solitary first card). There are seven of them. These cards will give you a general idea of "luck," or good fortune, for the coming month. See which suit appears the most in these seven. If it's Hearts, there will be a lot of luck. If it's Diamonds, quite a bit. Clubs, no more than usual. Spades, noticeable bad luck. Should you find that no one suit has more cards than the others, turn up more cards (in a separate pile) from the remaining cards, until

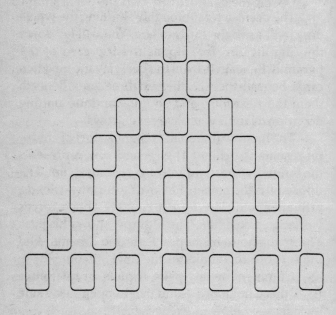

The Pyramid

one suit appears to match one of those tied.

2. *Sevens*

Using the deck of thirty-two, the client shuffles them and then cuts them with his left hand. From the top of the deck, count out seven cards. Discard the first six, as you count them, and lay the seventh face up on the table. Repeat this, counting seven more, discarding all but the last, which is placed beside the first one. Do this a third and a fourth time. Now take up the discarded cards and shuffle them in again with the cards you have left. Once again count out seven, discarding six and lay down the seventh. Repeat until you have twelve cards in all laid out on the table, face up, in a half circle. Study the cards to see if the Significator for your client is one of those cards face up. If it is not, then start over and do it until one of the twelve is the client's Significator.

Place the Significator in the center, above the line. Interpret the meaning of any pairs, triplets or quartettes there may be (see *Interpretation*, below).

Now count from the left of the line to the seventh card, and place this also above the line, next to the Significator. This seventh card is representative of the forces that have been working on the client in the past. Then take the two cards at the ends of the line—the one from the left and the other from the right—and pull them down below the line, placing them side by side. These represent the client's Hopes (left) and Fears (right). Again, count seven cards from the left along the remaining original line. Place this card down below the bottom two. This is a person whose influence will be coming into the client's life in the near future, for good or evil.

You now have seven cards left in the original line. Take the middle three of these and place them at the bottom. The four left in the original line are the forces now working all around the client, and the three pulled to the bottom are indicative of what the final outcome will be.

3. *Seven Times Two Plus Two*

This seems a longwinded way of saying "Sixteen," but the Gypsies put special significance on the number seven, hence *Seven Times Two Plus Two*.

After having well shuffled the deck of thirty-two, deal them out in two smaller decks, of sixteen cards each. Have the client choose one of these decks. Lay aside the top card, as a "surprise," and then turn up the other fifteen in a half-circle in front of you. If the Significator is not among them, start over, and repeat till it is one of the fifteen.

Now proceed to give a general reading from the cards, first by interpreting the meaning of any pairs, triplets, or quartettes among them; then by counting them in sevens, going from left to right, and reading those two (seventh) cards together; and finally by taking the cards at either extremity of the line and pairing them.

Next, gather up the fifteen cards, have the client shuffle and cut them, then deal them into three piles of five cards each. From each of these piles, withdraw the top card and place them on the "surprise" card you had put to one side. This now gives you four piles of four cards each, side by side on the table. Ask your client to choose one of these four piles. Turn it over and spread the cards. This is the set "For Himself." Take the pack furthest to your left and turn this up, below that first one. This is "His House." The third pack is laid out below that—"For Those Who Do Not Expect It" (i.e. unexpected events that are coming up). The fourth pack, laid out now at the bottom, is "The Surprise" (i.e. the final outcome).

4. Past, Present and Future

Have the client shuffle the deck of thirty-two cards. Take the top and bottom cards and lay them on one side as "the surprise." Deal out the remaining thirty cards in three piles: left, center and right. The left pile represents the past; the center, the present; the right pile, the future.

The piles are turned over and spread one at a time. They are interpreted, giving attention to any pairs, triplets and quartettes. Finally the "Surprise" cards are turned over. They represent unexpected forces which may come into play at any time.

5. Romani Star

This uses the deck of thirty-two cards. First pick out the Significator, then hand the balance of the deck to the client to shuffle. As usual, have him concentrate on any special question that needs to be answered.

Take the deck and count off the top eleven cards. These are discarded. The client reshuffles the balance and cuts them into two piles. You take off the top

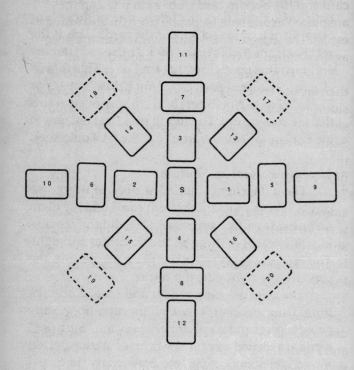

Romani Star

card and the bottom card from each pile and these are placed to one side (separate from the discarded cards). The sixteen cards which now remain are once again shuffled by the client and handed to you.

Lay the Significator in the center of the table, then lay out the chosen cards as follows: First card, sideways to the right of the Significator. Second, sideways to the left. Third, vertical, above the Significator. Fourth, vertical below. Fifth, vertical to the right, next to the First. Sixth, vertical to the left, next to the Second. Seventh, sideways above the Third. Eighth, sideways below the Fourth. Ninth, sideways, to the right, beside the Fifth. Tenth, sideways, to the left, beside the Sixth. Eleventh, vertical above the Seventh. Twelfth, vertical below the Eighth. The Thirteenth is placed diagonally in the top right quarter (between the Third and the First). The Fourteenth, diagonally in the top left quarter (between the Third and the Sixth). The Fifteenth, diagonally in the lower left quarter (between Second and Eighth). The Sixteenth, diagonally in the lower right quarter (between Fourth and First).

Start reading the cards in pairs, beginning with One and Two, followed by Three and Four. Then Five and Nine; Six and Ten; Seven and Eleven; Eight and Twelve; Thirteen and Fifteen; Fourteen and Sixteen. The cards closer to the Significator (e.g. One and Two) will, of course, have more effect on the client. Those further away (e.g. Six and Ten) will have less effect, though it may be that it is more a question of time, rather than immediate influence. In other words, those close to the Significator will be influencing him in the immediate future; those further away will influence in the further distant future. Only you will be able to tell this, from how you feel as you read the cards.

Having read these seventeen cards, take up the four that were set to one side and lay them down as follows: the First (I'll actually call it number Seventeen, to continue from the others we have laid down) is laid in the top right, sideways above number Thirteen. Eighteen is laid sideways in the top left, above Fourteen. Nineteen is laid sideways in the lower left, below Fifteen. And Twenty is laid sideways in the lower right, below Sixteen.

These last four cards are also read in pairs— Seventeen with Nineteen; Eighteen with Twenty. They represent the Final Outcome; the end to which all the other cards are leading.

One word on this layout, and on any similar layouts. With the significator and those laid down the same way, vertically, it is obvious when a card is reversed. Even with those on the diagonal you can tell. But with cards laying sideways, you can't immediately tell. All you need do is move slightly (or simply turn your head a little) to the left—as though you were sitting behind card number Ten—and look at the layout from that perspective, to study the sideways cards.

6. *The Nine Square*

This layout uses the full deck of fifty-two cards. First the Significator is removed, then the client shuffles the deck. He cuts them into two piles with his left hand. Remove the bottom card from each pile and discard it. The client rejoins the two piles and again shuffles. You then take the deck and deal out three piles of five cards each. The next card is laid, face down, to one side. This is known as the "Surprise." Now deal off a second row of three piles of five cards, immediately below the first row. Again lay aside the next card, face down, in the Surprise pile. Now lay out a third row below the other two, of five cards to a pile.

This should leave you with just two cards. The top one you place with the others in the Surprise pile. The remaining card you turn face up in front of you. If its suit is Hearts, you pick up piles One, Five and Nine, and discard the other piles. If the suit is Diamonds, pick piles Three, Five and Seven. If Clubs, piles Two, Five and Eight. And if Spades, pick piles Four, Five and Six.

The Significator is now added to the three piles chosen, and all sixteen of these cards are shuffled by the client. Turn them face up and spread them, in a fan, across the table in front of you. These cards are the ones read, paying due attention to their closeness or distance from the Significator. Finally the Surprise cards are turned over. These are indicative of unexpected event(s) that are going to come into play in the near future.

7. *Cross of the Year*

This layout uses all fifty-two cards and is used for looking at the year ahead. The cards are arranged in twelve columns downwards, representing the

The Nine Square

twelve months of the year, and with columns across representing the four seasons.

No significator is used. The client shuffles the deck and then you lay them out in threes, one set below the other, for twelve rows. In line with the sixth and seventh rows, then lay two cards (one above the other) to the left; two to the right; two to the left; two to the right, and so on until all cards have been laid down.

As stated, the rows of three, in the vertical column downwards, represent the months; the first (top) row being January, second row February, and so on. From the arms of the cross, the first four cards (two outer columns on the far left of the main vertical) represent Spring, the second four (next to the main vertical) Summer, then the first four on the right Fall and the last four Winter.

The "months" are read first, then the "seasons" are consulted for additional information affecting the three months in that season.

8. *Lucky Thirteen*

Using the full deck of fifty-two cards, have the client shuffle them and then cut the deck into two parts, with the left hand, to the left. Take up the right-hand pile and count off thirteen cards from the top of it. These are the ones used in this reading (if this should be a very small pile, with less than thirteen cards, have the client shuffle and cut again).

Fan out the cards into a half circle. Interpret any double, triples, quartettes, and then read the cards in threes as follows. After reading the first three, let

Cross of the Year

the third card become the first card of the next three. Read those and again let the third card become the first of the next three, and so on. This will give six sets of threes in all.

This is a general reading covering coming events with, perhaps, a look at the present situation also. If the client has any particular question (which she should have been concentrating on whilst shuffling) the answer should be obvious in the cards. If, for any reason, it is not answered—or if she has another very urgent question, *related to the previous one*— then you may draw the card from the top of the left-hand pile (from the original cut made by the client) and that will hold the answer. This card should not be drawn, however, if it can be helped. It indicates only a *possibility* of what may come about.

There are many, many more layouts used by the Gypsies. It's impossible to include them all here; that would need a separate book. The ones I have included, above, seem to be particular favorites and are found in many areas of the country. As I mentioned above, many of the layouts for the tarot cards can be used equally well for regular playing cards.

INTERPRETATION

Most Gypsies give their own interpretation to the cards depending, of course, on the individual for whom they are reading. However, there does seem to be a lot of agreement on general interpretation (the Ace of Hearts—a love letter; the Ace of Clubs— prosperity, for example). I therefore include here a listing for all fifty-two cards, plus interpretation of pairs, triplets and quartettes—two, three or four cards of the same value, following one another.

Lucky Thirteen

HEARTS

Ace: A love letter, or some other pleasant news. *Reversed:* A visit from a friend.

King: A fair, liberal man. *Reversed:* A meeting with disappointment.

Queen: A mild, amiable woman. *Reversed:* Possibility of having been crossed in love.

Jack: A carefree bachelor who thinks only of pleasure. *Reversed:* A discontented man, possibly connected with the military.

Ten: Triumph; happiness. *Reversed:* Slight anxiety.

Nine: Satisfaction; joy; success. *Reversed:* A passing annoyance.

Eight: A fair person's affection. *Reversed:* Indifference.

Seven: Pleasant thoughts; tranquility. *Reversed:* Tedium; weariness; boredom.

Six: A sea voyage; good luck. *Reversed:* Sudden change of fortune.

Five: Dreams of great significance. *Reversed:* Jealousy.

Four: An engagement to be wed. *Reversed:* Difficulty in choosing between two lovers.

Three: Trust to your instincts. *Reversed:* Danger of trouble through lack of prudence.

Two: Great success. *Reversed:* Exercise caution in business dealings.

DIAMONDS

(*Note:* it is necessary to make a small mark on the cards of this suit to be able to tell whether or not they are reversed)

Ace: A letter soon to be received. *Reversed:* A letter containing bad news.

King: A fair man who can be cunning and dangerous. *Reversed:* A very great threat caused by him.

Queen: An ill-bred, scandal-loving woman. *Reversed:* She is to be feared.

Jack: An unfaithful friend or employee. *Reversed:* Many problems caused by him.

Ten: A relocation of home or business; a journey. *Reversed:* The change, or journey, will not be for the better.

Nine: Delay, with resultant annoyance. *Reversed:* A quarrel with your family, or lover.

Eight: An attempt to make love. *Reversed:* The attempt thwarted.

Seven: Satire; mockery. *Reversed:* A foolish scandal.

Six: Unhappy ends to a marriage. *Reversed:* Loss of your possessions.

Five: Children bringing joy; prosperity in business. *Reversed:* An unexpected financial loss.

Four: Trouble and aggravations. *Reversed:* Loss of a friend or good employee.

Three: Disputes and arguments, in the home and office. *Reversed:* A law suit.

Two: A love affair; a close friendship developing. *Reversed:* Scandal, loss of a friend.

CLUBS

Ace: Joy, prosperity or good news. *Reversed:* The joy will be of brief duration.

King: A frank, liberal man, fond of serving his friends. *Reversed:* He will meet with disappointment.

Queen: An affectionate, quick-witted woman. *Reversed:* Jealousy and maliciousness.

Jack: A clever and enterprising young man. *Reversed:* A harmless flirt and flatterer.

Ten: Fortune, success and fame. *Reversed:* Need for success.

Nine: A legacy; unexpected gain. *Reversed:* A disappointingly small gift received.

Eight: A dark person's affections. If returned, they will result in great prosperity. *Reversed:* An unwanted suitor.

Seven: A small debt repaid to you. *Reversed:* An even smaller amount received; disappointment.

Six: Hard work resulting in prosperity. *Reversed:* Hard work with little or no return.

Five: Good prospects for the future; a possible

wedding. *Reversed:* Plans coming to nothing.

Four: A change of fortune; impending evil. *Reversed:* Sudden and unexpected bad luck.

Three: Wealthy connections, possibly through marriage. *Reversed:* Loss of income.

Two: A disappointment. *Reversed:* Opposition to your desires.

SPADES

Ace: An emotional relationship that could cause trouble. *Reversed:* Unexpected bad news.

King: The envious man; an enemy, or dishonest lawyer, who is to be feared. *Reversed:* Impotence; malice.

Queen: A widow. *Reversed:* A dangerous and malicious woman.

Jack: A dark, ill-bred, young man. *Reversed:* He is plotting aginst you.

Ten: Grief; prison; restraint. *Reversed:* Brief affliction.

Nine: News of a death. *Reversed:* The death of a near relative.

Eight: Approaching illness. *Reversed:* A broken (marriage) engagement; an offer refused.

Seven: Many annoyances. *Reversed:* Foolish intrigue.

Six: Good plans and intentions meeting with failure. *Reversed:* Lack of ideas and plans.

Five: Quarreling brought about by short tempers. *Reversed:* Bickering, petty annoyances.

Four: Being passed over for promotion; missed opportunities. *Reversed:* Jealousy and envy.

Three: Faithlessness in love; bitterness. *Reversed:* News of indiscretions.

Two: Separation; change. *Reversed:* Unwanted and unexpected change.

PAIRS, TRIPLETS, AND QUARTETTES

In the thirty-two card decks, two, three or four cards of the same denomination, coming together, have special meaning as follows:

Aces

Four Aces: danger, failure in business; sometimes imprisonment. If one or more of them is *reversed*, the danger is lessened.

Three Aces: Good tidings. One or more *reversed:* Folly.

Two Aces; A plot. *Reversed:* It is unsuccessful.

Kings

Four Kings: Rewards, dignities, honors. *Reversed:* These will be less but will be received sooner.

Three Kings: A consultation on important business, with very satisfactory results. *Reversed:* Doubtful success.

Two Kings: A partnership in business. *Reversed:* A partnership dissolved.

Queens

Four Queens: Company; society. *Reversed:* Things

will not go well.

Three Queens: Friendly calls. *Reversed:* Scandal and deceit; gossip.

Two Queens: A meeting between friends. *Reversed:* Trouble, in which one will involve the other.

Jacks

Four Jacks: A noisy party, mostly young people. *Reversed:* A drinking bout.

Three Jacks: False friends. *Reversed:* A quarrel with someone beneath you.

Two Jacks: Evil intentions. *Reversed:* Danger.

Tens

Four Tens: Great success in plans. *Reversed:* The success won't be so great but it will still be sure.

Three Tens: Improper conduct. *Reversed:* Failure.

Two Tens: Change of profession. *Reversed:* This is only a distant possibility.

Nines

Four Nines: A great surprise. *Reversed:* A celebration.

Three Nines: Joy, fortune, good health. *Reversed:* Wealth lost by imprudence.

Two Nines: A small gain. *Reversed:* Small losses through gambling.

Eights

Four Eights: A short journey. Reversed: The return of a friend or relative.

Three Eights: Thoughts of marriage. *Reversed:*

Flirtation, foolishness.
Two Eights: A brief dream of love. *Reversed:* Small pleasure and minor pain.

Sevens

Four Sevens: Intrigue among low people; threats, snares and disputes. *Reversed:* The harm will fall back on the perpetrators.
Three Sevens: Sickness, premature old age. *Reversed:* Slight and brief indisposition.
Two Sevens: Levity. *Reversed:* Regret.

Any picture (Court) card between two others of equal value (e.g. a Queen between two sevens) indicates that the person represented by that picture card (as a Significator) runs the risk of being caught up in a conflict.

Interestingly, some Romanies in the north of England use rhymes to go with the card meanings. I tend to think that these are usually given when the client simply cuts the deck to turn up one card, for a quick fortune. Most of these rhymes seem to be aimed at women clients.

HEARTS

Ace   "Your fate is sealed on a Friday night,
'Midst music, song and pure delight."

King   "A lover true now waits for you.
Don't say 'No' whate'er you do."

Queen   "The Queen of Hearts, the King of Love,
A ring, a rose, and a silken glove."

Jack   "Beware of Cupid and his darts!
          Your fate is held by the Knave of Hearts."

Ten   "Triumph in all things near at hand.
          Spread the good word thoughout the land."

Nine   "A whisper of love, a whisper of hate,
          Tie a silk thread to the garden gate."

Eight "A twilight kiss and a dream of bliss—
          A little black dog will lead you to this."

Seven "On Tuesday you may look to find
          A lover who is true and kind."

Six   "If a blue butterfly you see,
          It is your luck to go over the sea."

Five   "Five this week's your lucky number,
          and fortune comes to you in slumber."

Four   "As you sit in the firelight glow,
          His name is writ in the embers low."

Three "The third hour of the third day.
          The King of Hearts shall win you away."

Two   "The viper's tongue, the sting of lies,
          Beyond dark clouds are blue, blue skies."

DIAMONDS

Ace   "A song of love, a kiss that burns,
          And your luck on the Ace of Diamond
          turns."

King   "When bees in honeysuckle sip,
          Love shall be sealed with a scarlet lip."

Queen "This week or next will likely bring
          Good luck and an engagement ring."

Jack   "A butterfly wing set in a ring,
This to you good luck should bring."

Ten   "A change of view, a sense of waste,
A change of residence in haste."

Nine   "Two days from now, take care what you
say,
'Twill bind you for five years and a day."

Eight   "Should you doubt his love for you,
Place a golden bead in your left shoe."

Seven   "Three men, three men in love with you.
The first and last will ne'er be true."

Six   "If you would be a rich man's wife,
Cut a silken cord with a silver knife."

Five   "If a large black cat you see,
'Twill bring good luck 'twixt one and three."

Four   "Under your pillow, place a rose.
For luck to your lover where'er he goes."

Three   "Three words of love in a garden fair—
He shall be waiting for you there."

Two   "A spider spinning on the wall
Shows he'll be brave, and strong, and tall."

CLUBS

Ace   "Two hearts entwined on the trunk of a
tree—
The man who cut it is true to thee."

King   "A kiss within an hour of noon
Will bring a wedding very soon."

Queen "A lover's knot that none shall break,
Two shall ask, the third shall take."

Jack "Two eyes of blue and hair like gold,
And two strong arms about you fold."

Ten "Wednesday for fortune is the day,
So be prepared, let fate point the way."

Nine "Love, wealth and happiness will be yours,
If every night you lock three doors."

Eight "Someone is waiting, someone you know,
You will have luck when you meet in the
snow."

Seven "His words are fair, his heart is black,
So turn to one whose name is Jack."

Six "The six of clubs will bring you hope.
Make three knots in a piece of rope."

Five "If when the moon is full you kiss,
It will lead to married bliss."

Four "A Gypsy woman will tell you the truth—
You are fated to marry the love of your
youth."

Three "Wealth, good health, and a lover true,
These are the three in store for you."

Two "The Priest of Isis scans your fate—
Your true love waits at the old church gate."

SPADES

Ace "If hearts be true, then naught can stay
Love's arrow on a coming day."

King	"When Friday dawns a golden morn, You'll thank the stars that you were born."
Queen	"A kitten, a kitten as white as snow, By her tomorrow your luck you'll know."
Jack	"If his name begins with G, You will ever happy be."
Ten	"Ten long days, till set of sun, Behind jail bars; you cannot run."
Nine	"For love and luck, when the sun goes down, Rub a new penny and change your gown."
Eight	"At ten in the morning on Wednesday, You will be traveling far away."
Seven	"Your lucky color is apple green. And your lucky number, twice fourteen."
Six	"His heart is gold, his eyes are grey, You'll meet him twice on Saturday."
Five	"On a summer's day, by the deep blue sea, You'll have luck if you count to fifty-three."
Four	"A letter written in purple ink, Will bring you more than you can think."
Three	"Queen of his heart you'll ever reign, If you should meet him in a train."
Two	"Though sorrow come with parting pain, He shall come back to you again."

Va A la spera del Sole di fuorisi fiume io rdano	Va A la spera di fiume Nera	Va A la spera del Venus di fuori si fiume Petinera	Va A la spera del fiume Per o	Va A la spera del fiume Caspente	Va A la spera del fiume fiamo
Va A la spera de Saturno di fuorisi fiume Rodano	Va A la spera del Capricorno di fuori di fiume Ticinio	Va A la spera de Marte di fuori al fiume carpento	Va A la spera de Aquario di fiume Alfiume Peio	Va A la spera del Lunadi fuori al fiume fario	Va A la spera del falcone di fuori al Cruo
Va A al spera de Venus di fuori Al spera di spera Fiume Eufrates di fuori di	Va A la spera del fiume Alfiume	Va A la spera del Aquario di fuori al fiume digmo	Va A la spera de Aquario di fuori al mercurio di fuori al fiume amignon	Va a la spera del sole di fuori al fiume Ciudra
Va A la spera del Sole di fuori Al fiume Marechta	Va A la spera de Aquario di fuori Alfiume Tebro	Va A la spera e Mercurio di fuori Al fiume	Va A la spera del fiume	Va A la spera del fiume di fuori Al fiume Iuno	Va a la spera de Saturno di fuori al fiume

Va A la spera de Marte di fuori Al fiume celson	Va A la spera e colore di fuori Al fiume Nilo		Va A la spera del Pauone di fuori Al fiume Ilo	Va A la spera di di fuori al fiume Osoep
Va A la spera de la Luna di fuori Al fiume Arma	Va A la spera del falcone di fuori Al fiume Adice		Va A la spera del monte one di fuori al fiume Reina	Va la spera e marte di fuori al fiume alpha
Va A la spera de Mercurio di fuori Al fiume Teuere	Va A la spera del Sole di fuori Al fiume ch Lacio	Va A la spera del tauro di fuori Al fiume Stretto	Va A la spera del Falcone di fuori Al fiume cesio	Va A la spera del Lunaia di fuori Alfiume vius	Va A la spera e luna di fuori al fiume tno
Va a la spera de Tauro di fuori Al fiume Po	Va A la spera de Saturno di fuori Al fiume Raluo	Va A la spera del Pauone di fuori al fiume terso	Va A la spera della sole di fuori Al fiume marechia	Va A la spera del cariso no di fuori Alfiume Rasa	Va la spera e di fuori al fiume ido
Va a la spera del Pauone di fuori al fiume Patenza	Va A la spera del sole di fuori al fiume Deiso	Va A la spera del monne di fuori al fiume tonto	Va A la spera de saturno di fuori Al fiume tronto	Va A la spera de tag tario di fuori Al fiume vilo	Va la spera e di fuori al fiume
Va a la spera del Montone di fuori al fiume chiente	Va A la spera del Saturno di fuori A.Fiume Meluno	Va A la spera de Orsula di fuori Al fiume talo	Va A la spera de Venus di fuori Al fiume Deijho	Va a la spera de Aquario di fuori al fiume Italo	Va A la spera al di fuori al fiume gosa

A.

DICE

Having studied the most popular forms of *dukkerin'* used by the Romani, let's look now at some of the other methods of telling fortunes. Most of them use very simple, basic tools. A good example is dice. Many a *Rom* will carry a set of dice in his pocket. They are less cumbersome than a deck of cards . . . and less obvious.

In different parts of England there are variations found in the interpretations given to the dice, but on the whole they seem to follow the same pattern. Basically, the throw of the dice (three of them) gives an answer to your question(s). The answer, or prophesy, is said to come true within nine days. Here is the simplest method of using them.

Mark a chalk circle (or scratch it in the dirt of the ground) about twelve inches in diameter. The three dice should be held in the right hand, by the Querent, and he should concentrate on his question. Then, in complete silence, he cups them in both hands and gives them a good shake. He then throws the dice into the circle. Any die or dice that roll out of the circle are disregarded. If all of them roll out, this foretells a quarrel or an estrangement, and you must throw again. If all of them roll out a second time, then no fortune can be told that day.

Of those that stay in the circle, add the numbers that show. Their meaning is as follows:

One—Loneliness; loss.
Two—Love or infatuation.
Three—A pleasant surprise is coming.
Four—An unpleasant surprise.
Five—You will meet with a stranger who will have a strong influence on you.
Six—You will lose something you value.
Seven—There will be a scandal involving you.
Eight—A wrong that you did in the past will catch up with you.
Nine—There is a wedding in the near future.
Ten—Business advancement.
Eleven—The death of someone you know.
Twelve—You will soon receive a letter of some importance.
Thirteen—There will be cause for you to weep.
Fourteen—A new admirer.
Fifteen—Be especially cautious; trouble threatens.
Sixteen—A happy journey.
Seventeen—Profitable business is coming to you from across water.
Eighteen—Some very great good is coming to you.

There is a second way of using the dice. This is

the method usually used by a "Fortune Teller," or Dukkerer, at a fairground. Just two dice are used and there is a set list of questions ("Three questions answered for $2!"). These questions may be written down, but it is far more likely that the Dukkerer has them in her head and, whatever question the client asks of her, she can apply it to one of these set questions. They certainly seem to cover most contingencies.

The client will hold the two dice in her right hand for a moment while she concentrates on her question. She will then state the question out loud (for the benefit of the interpreter—you) and throw the dice down on the table. There is no circle to throw them into, as in the previous example. You simply give the answer according to the upturned faces of the two dice.

As an example, suppose the client asks "Will my secret be discovered?" and then throws down a five and a two. The question is number 17. The answer to number seventeen, for a five and a two, is "Nobody thinks of asking about it." It can be seen that a large number of questions can be asked and answered in this way.

QUESTIONS

1. Does the person I love think of me often?
2. Will anyone soon date me?
3. What must I do to please my love?
4. Shall I answer?
5. Shall I agree to what is asked of me?

6. How many admirers will I have?
7. How many times will I be married?
8. What sort of person will my spouse be?
9. What does s/he think of me?
10. May I trust her/him?
11. Does s/he love me?
12. Does s/he think that I love her/him?
13. Will my heart remain free much longer?
14. Shall I soon get married?
15. Shall I experience many adventures?
16. Shall I be rich?
17. Will my secret be discovered?
18. Am I thought to be good looking?
19. Am I thought to be discreet, witty, and interesting?
20. Will I marry the person I am thinking of?
21. Shall I do it?
22. Shall I see my love again soon?
23. Shall I soon receive a letter?
24. Which of the two shall I choose?
25. Shall I soon receive a present?
26. Shall I soon make a journey?
27. Will my condition shortly be changed?
28. Will my wish be fulfilled?
29. What is s/he doing at present?
30. What will my husband be?
31. Will it prove a blessing to me?
32. Shall I soon receive the news I'm waiting for?

ANSWERS

TWO

1. They think of you as much as you think of them.
2. Tomorrow morning, about eleven o'clock.
3. Whatever you do, do it gracefully and especially always treat them with respect.
4. Yes, but word your reply discreetly.
5. No. You must not.
6. A dozen at least!
7. One.
8. Young, slender, and fair complexioned.
9. That you are a very special person.
10. No, you may not, for they are not good at heart.
11. S/he cannot help her/himself.
12. You have shown it plainly enough.
13. You know very well that it has not been free this long while!
14. In a week.
15. Your life will be as peaceful as a quiet lake.
16. You will always have all you need.
17. It would be a good thing if it were discovered.
18. All except your nose.
19. Discreet indeed, but not witty, and only interesting at times!
20. No.
21. Why not?
22. Tomorrow.

23. Not as soon as you would wish.
24. The one who has the longest nose.
25. Very soon, and it will be a kiss.
26. Yes. A very long one.
27. Yes, to your joy and happiness.
28. It will.
29. Busy attending to her/his own affairs.
30. Very rich.
31. It will lead to the greatest happiness.
32. Sooner than you expect.

THREE

1. Not in the least.
2. Much too soon, as it will turn out.
3. Always dress well. Never have bare arms unless absolutely necessary.
4. It is hazardous.
5. Yes, without the slighest fear.
6. As many admirers as you will have spouses.
7. Twice.
8. Fat and round as a ball. But of a very sweet disposition.
9. That you have stolen her/his heart.
10. Have you not already had enough proof of this?
11. S/he is yours, heart and soul.
12. S/he has doubts.
13. Tomorrow, when you first go out, you will meet someone who will become very special to you.

14. In two years.
15. Your life will move along like a foaming torrent.
16. As rich as you are at present.
17. No, but it would be good to disclose it as soon as possible.
18. When you are pleasant and friendly, but not when you are ill-tempered.
19. To one person at least, very interesting.
20. If you really want her/him.
21. If you wish; it will do no harm.
22. Within three weeks.
23. Yes, but not the one you had hoped for.
24. The darker one.
25. Yes.
26. You will soon be seeing cities you never expected to see.
27. When you shall wish it changed.
28. If it is really your wish.
29. Looking through books and papers.
30. An engineer.
31. No, that's impossible.
32. Not for quite a while.

FOUR

1. Always.
2. Aren't you always surrounded by admirers?
3. Treat her/him with frankness and honesty.
4. It would be better if you didn't.
5. Yes, but do it prudently.

6. Five.
7. Once, to a very jealous person.
8. Loving and tender.
9. That you are very hard-hearted.
10. You don't need to mistrust too much.
11. Can't you tell from her/his face?
12. Hopes so, but has many doubts.
13. At five o'clock tomorrow afternoon, love's arrow will strike!
14. In six weeks.
15. Many thrilling adventures.
16. Quite wealthy.
17. It will unless you are always on your guard.
18. Quite attractive.
19. Reasonably so.
20. Yes.
21. If it will give you pleasure.
22. No, you are separated forever.
23. There is one on the way right now.
24. The one who always gazes upon you with such a shrewd expression.
25. Yes, but from someone different from the one you thought.
26. A short, sentimental one.
27. Yes, but you won't benefit from it.
28. If you do everything you can to bring it about.
30. Very spiritual.
31. It will bring you both joy and sorrow.
32. Never.

FOUR

1. Are you not fascinating?
2. Yes, but be careful. It is a rogue who will be next.
3. Show a little more kindness to other human beings.
4. Frankly and without affectation.
5. It would be too cruel to refuse.
6. Only one. But that one will admire you more than all others put together.
7. Once.
8. Very homely, but in your eyes very handsome.
9. That it would be dangerous to trust you.
10. Oh, yes. With all your heart.
11. Haven't you noticed how s/he blushes when looking at you?
12. Without a doubt.
13. At the next social event you attend, your heart will be touched.
14. Never.
15. Too many by far.
16. You'll have so much wealth you won't know what to do with it.
17. It is discovered already.
18. Not greatly so, but somewhat.
19. Mischievous.
20. Yes, and others.
21. Do what you can't help doing.
22. Very soon.
23. The one you would like to receive, you will never receive.

24. The one with the long hair.
25. Very soon.
26. Yes. One that you are looking forward to.
27. It will depend entirely on yourself.
28. It will. Certainly.
29. Dining with someone else.
30. A lawyer.
31. It will bring you joy and happiness.
32. Perhaps within the year.

FIVE

1. They would like to but dare not.
2. When you stop worrying about it.
3. Show your appreciation of their friendship.
4. It would never do to keep silent.
5. You can't do otherwise.
6. Four; possibly five.
7. Once, and it will be the joy of your life. Name begins with a "G."
8. Very tall with a light complexion. Wears spectacles and is very friendly to everyone.
9. That s/he can neither understand your actions nor your words.
10. You can believe what s/he says and discount the gossip.
11. You can find that out next time you pass her/him a drink. If, in taking it, s/he touches your hand, then there is love.
12. Yes, and is flattered by it.

13. At the moment your heart is *not* free. Examine it.
14. Within a year.
15. Very many. Mostly with rogues and robbers.
16. Rich in love and friendship, but not in money.
17. You think that it's a secret but it never has been one.
18. Passably so.
19. You are thought to be capricious.
20. It's very doubtful.
21. It will do no good, and no harm.
22. If you send an invitation, otherwise no.
23. Very soon, a very tender one.
24. The one who first reaches out to touch you.
25. Yes, a living one.
26. Yes, but not the one you're presently thinking of.
27. Not so very soon.
28. Yes, but not as soon as you'd like.
29. Sleeping.
30. A doctor.
31. Only so long as you keep your heart pure and true.
32. Yes, in a few hours.

FIVE

1. They are far too busy with other things to keep thinking of you!
2. If you would treat a certain person with a little more regard they would be happy to do so.

3. Don't pay so much attention to others.
4. Answer as it deserves to be answered.
5. Follow your heart.
6. Many, but most of them you'll find boring.
7. Once, to a very unromantic person whose name begins with a "B."
8. Very tall and of dark complexion; somewhat quarrelsome, jealous, but with the best of intentions.
9. That it would be very dangerous to see you often.
10. Inquire what others say about her/him. There is a lot of truth in what is said.
11. With heart and soul.
12. Since the last time you were together, s/he is sure of it.
13. You know very well that right now you are in love.
14. In five months.
15. No. Very few.
16. You will have money, which is not necessarily the same as being rich.
17. If you tell no one . . . no.
18. If you could be a little less self-conscious you would be thought so.
19. Many people think you a genius but, because of that, think you have many faults.
20. Yes, you will.
21. Certainly not!
22. At a time when you least expect it.
23. Yes, and it will make you very happy.
24. The one with the largest hands.

25. Not soon.
26. Yes, the one you are thinking of.
27. Not in the way you wish.
28. Yes, and sooner than you expect.
29. Arguing with someone.
30. Connected with science.
31. Yes, though it won't appear so at first.
32. Within three days . . . or never.

SIX

1. As often as circumstances permit.
2. You will have wrinkles before that happens to you!
3. Don't be so terribly affected. Try to be more natural.
4. Yes, just as your heart prompts you.
5. Be very careful. You might be laughed at.
6. Seven, at least.
7. Once, to a dear, good and amiable person.
8. Friendly and cheerful, of a romantic turn, somewhat poetical, but just a trifle weak.
9. That you are the guiding star of her/his existence.
10. You can tell by looking into those honest eyes.
11. Only as a brother or sister would.
12. If you keep giving those tender glances s/he can hardly doubt it.
13. At the moment you love one, but you will soon love another.
14. Within four years.

15. Your life will be a very weary one.
16. If you are careful and watch your money.
17. There is one person who knows it but will not tell it.
18. Some think so . . . others do not.
19. You are generally thought to be heartless and soulless.
20. You know yourself that is impossible.
21. Think what your family would say.
22. Yes, in the not too far distant future.
23. Yes, but it will bring sad news.
24. The one who blushes most often.
25. You must be patient for a while.
26. Not as soon as you hope.
27. Very soon, and in a particular way.
28. It will be fulfilled, but not completely and not quite as you had hoped.
29. Spending time with an older person of the opposite sex.
30. A merchant.
31. If you take it as it is meant.
32. Probably within a month.

SIX

1. Yes, as well you know.
2. Yes, but they won't be serious about it.
3. Do not be over-sweet.
4. It would be best if you did.
5. Yes, if you can do it without blushing.
6. Two; one dark and one fair.

7. More than once, and none of them good.
8. A small person, full of conceit and vanity.
9. That you are as near perfect as possible.
0. It is well to be prudent.
1. Yes, but s/he also loves many others.
2. Not exactly, but s/he thinks it would be easy to win your heart.
3. For a year yet, but no longer.
4. In six years. No sooner, no matter how hard you try.
5. Many but none especially interesting.
6. You will have plenty of money, but if you or your spouse should gamble you will lose it all.
7. You will betray yourself.
8. A lot of people think you homely, some few think you pretty, and one or two think you beautiful.
9. You are thought to be quick at repartee but not really witty.
0. Yes, if you succeed in winning her/his heart within two weeks.
1. Do it, even though there is someone it will greatly displease.
2. You will have to wait awhile.
3. Yes, a very long one.
4. The more modest of the two.
5. Very soon, and one which will delight you.
6. Yes, but one that will cost you many tears.
7. Soon, and by an unexpected occurrence.
8. Yes, and more fully than you have reason to expect.
9. Preparing witticisms to speak in your presence.

30. A broker.
31. It will cost you many tears at first, but will end up well.
32. Very soon.

SIX

1. Thinking of you now and very tenderly.
2. Quite a number.
3. Work on your hair.
4. Place a poppy under your pillow tonight and you will dream of what you should do.
5. Ask advice of your closest friend.
6. One older man, who you won't care for.
7. Twice.
8. A person of strong character; high minded and energetic, with wit and humor also.
9. That you have broken many hearts.
10. No one better deserves confidence.
11. S/he is a true friend to you, that is all.
12. S/he has never thought about it at all.
13. It will always be free enough.
14. Very soon.
15. Many, and most of them interesting.
16. If you keep from speculating.
17. If you can refrain from babbling!
18. If you didn't wrinkle your nose when you laugh you would be better looking.
19. Some people think you peculiar, but there are a few who really understand you.
20. If you can truly love them.

21. Yes, it will give you great pleasure.
22. Not until you both have grey hairs.
23. Not soon, but when you do it will be a very tender one.
24. The least pretentious one.
25. At the moment no one is thinking of giving you anything.
26. One which will give you much pleasure.
27. Soon, and in a way you would never have dreamed of.
28. Sooner than you expect.
29. Sighing over the low state of her/his finances.
30. A farmer.
31. If you can always stay cheerful and optimisitc.
32. You should know when you may expect it.

SEVEN

1. Yes, and regrets it.
2. Congratulate yourself if they don't, for there are few worth having.
3. Don't get so sentimental, don't talk so much, and try to use a little more common sense.
4. What is spoken vanishes; what is written remains.
5. You may grant all that is asked for nothing unworthy will be requested.
6. Over twenty, five of whom are already in love with you.
7. Three times.

8. A large person in love with him/herself.
9. That you would like to bring her/him to despair.
10. Consult your best female friend about this.
11. Her/his heart has long belonged to another and s/he would never be unfaithful.
12. No but s/he thinks how pleasant it would be if you did.
13. Your heart is free at present but won't be for much longer.
14. Not until you love a certain person more tenderly than you do at present.
15. Yes, and they will prove too exciting for you.
16. So long as you make good use of the money.
17. No, it will not.
18. If you wear more subdued clothing and improve your complexion.
19. Discreet but very vain and proud.
20. Yes, if they are not already engaged.
21. Of course. You would be a fool not to.
22. Not very soon.
23. Yes, and the paper will be wet with tears.
24. The one with the larger ears.
25. Someone will offer you one but you would do well to reject it.
26. An important and joyful occurrence will prevent it.
27. Not very soon.
28. That will depend on you. Act prudently.
29. Hurrying to see you.
30. A government worker.
31. If you can keep your presence of mind.
32. Not for some time.

SEVEN

1. All the time.
2. Yes, but it won't bring you happiness.
3. Just enjoy life; relax and be yourself.
4. Without hesitation.
5. Go to your mother for advice.
6. Two. One's initial is "L."
7. Only once.
8. Young and handsome, with rosy cheeks.
9. That you have been deceitful.
10. Yes, but not too far.
11. From the moment you first met.
12. S/he thinks that at least you would like to love her/him.
13. The next journey you take you will fall in love.
14. Within two years.
15. Some pleasant ones, and kind friends will protect you from unpleasant ones.
16. No, never.
17. Nobody even thinks of enquiring about it.
18. Yes.
19. You are thought to be thoroughly charming.
20. You would, if it were not for a false friend.
21. Certainly. You can't do better.
22. S/he is working on how to bring that about.
23. A very foolish one quite soon.
24. The one with the large mouth.
25. A splendid one, very soon.
26. You will have the opportunity, though you

may not take it.
27. Yes, in the way you expect.
28. It will be your own fault if it's not.
29. Practicing what s/he is to say to you.
30. A professional person.
31. It will be the prelude to the fulfillment of your warmest wishes.
32. You will soon receive it and shed tears of joy.

SEVEN

1. Yes, but not in the way you would like.
2. You will soon have more than you can accept.
3. Get a good sun tan.
4. Yes, but make it clear you are not happy about it.
5. Only in part.
6. Many, but few of them attractive.
7. If you accepted all that offered it would be twenty-five times at least!
8. Tall and thin as a beanpole.
9. "You do not deserve my love."
10. Fully and frankly.
11. Yes, but resists it thinking you do not return the love.
12. Not that you truly love, just that you are a little smitten.
13. It will be a long time before you give away your heart.
14. Within the year.
15. No.

16. Gold will rain down upon you.
17. You had better be on your guard or it will leak out.
18. Don't think about it.
19. Good natured enough but rather vain.
20. If you would flirt less with others s/he would be a lot more interested in you.
21. People will laugh at you but don't let that stop you.
22. It will only happen by accident.
23. Yes, but you won't understand it.
24. The one who agrees with you.
25. Yes, one with which you will be delighted.
26. A sad occurrence will prevent it.
27. Yes, but not in the way you expect.
28. Wicked people will prevent it.
29. Thinking how boring life can be.
30. A literary person.
31. It will give you initial pleasure but later tears.
32. Yes, and you know who it will be from.

EIGHT

1. Frequently.
2. Yes, a plain looking person with a good sense of humor.
3. Pay a little more attention to them.
4. Answer what your heart dictates.
5. No.
6. About a dozen.

7. Once, or possibly not at all.
8. A great favorite, especially of the opposite sex.
9. That you don't like her/him.
10. Has s/he ever done anything to make you distrust her/him?
11. With great longing.
12. Did so once but no longer.
13. In about six weeks, by starlight, your heart will be softened.
14. In a year or two.
15. A reasonable number.
16. Labor always to be rich in contentment of mind.
17. It is half discovered already.
18. Absolutely beautiful.
19. In every respect.
20. No, so don't expect to.
21. If you don't, you're lost.
22. In a few weeks.
23. Yes, in eight days.
24. The one who gives you a gift.
25. One which you will soon wish you never got.
26. Yes, in the company of someone of the opposite sex.
27. In a very agreeable manner.
28. An unexpected accident will prevent it.
29. Contemplating a change of job/lifestyle.
30. A business person.
31. If you are strong enough to suppress all vanity.
32. Not as soon as you'd like; there will be a wait.

EIGHT

1. More than you think of them.
2. No one worthy of having.
3. Not eat so heartily.
4. There's no danger in it.
5. If you do you will bring joy to one heart and break another.
6. Two, both good looking.
7. Once, and that will be one too many.
8. A drunkard and a gambler.
9. "S/he has caused me so much suffering I can never forgive her/him."
10. Yes, but keep your wits about you.
11. As much as possible, but that may not be much.
12. No. S/he thinks your feelings are those of a brother or sister.
13. Is your heart really your own now?
14. Within three years.
15. Only a few.
16. You will have gold by the bushel.
17. Not if you are discreet.
18. You roll your eyes too much, your ears are not well shaped, but your hands are well formed.
19. More or less so.
20. You don't really wish it.
21. If you are prudent it can do no harm.
22. By the end of next summer.
23. Not the one you wish. That will be delayed.
24. The one who is polite and well mannered.
25. Yes, over which you will shed tears of joy.

26. Very soon, and in pleasant company.
27. Yes, and exactly to your wishes.
28. It will, and it will bring you great happiness.
29. Counting the hours till seeing you again.
30. A mechanic.
31. Everything is a blessing. Sometimes we mis-interpret.
32. Not soon. Don't be impatient.

EIGHT

1. Don't expect too much.
2. The first person you meet tomorrow.
3. Argue with her/him a little, but not too much.
4. Yes, but choose your words carefully.
5. Ask the advice of a close relative.
6. One. A slow, fair-haired person with a large mouth.
7. As many times as you have already had lovers.
8. Attractive and in the prime of life.
9. That you are amusing.
10. Trust no one blindly in this world.
11. Yes, and hopes that it is returned.
12. S/he thinks that you are dying of love for her/him.
13. You have already been in love a dozen times. You may be another dozen.
14. In three to four years.
15. Storms and calms by the score.
16. You will never want, so long as you remain industrious.

17. No, but by keeping it secret you will bring upon yourself many disagreeable consequences.
18. You would look better if you smiled more often.
19. Witty and amusing.
20. If not it will be through no fault of your own.
21. Yes, but as quietly as possible.
22. At the next party you attend.
23. Not for a long time.
24. The one with the soft eyes.
25. Very soon, from the one you love.
26. Yes, and it will have a decisive effect on your life.
27. If you act prudently in a critical moment which is at hand, it will.
28. Yes, and you'll wish it hadn't been.
29. Writing a love letter.
30. A politician.
31. If it happens without your interference, it will cause much happiness to you.
32. It will come one day, but not yet.

NINE

1. Only as one thinks of a small, insignificant creature.
2. Yes, a sailor. But this sailor is heir to a fortune.
3. Do what is asked of you.
4. No! It would turn out very badly.
5. Better not to, though it would do no real harm.
6. Three; one rich and two poor.

7. Once, to someone who will remain completely under your thumb.
8. A wearying person, with little energy.
9. That you are fairly attractive and that if s/he could love anyone, it would be you.
10. Although a flirt, towards you the intentions are honorable.
11. You are her/his first and only love.
12. S/he imagines it's possible, at times, because s/he desperately wants it to be so.
13. For at least two more years.
14. Within five years.
15. When you are traveling, not any other time.
16. If you always watch the pennies.
17. Nothing is so carefully hidden that it doesn't eventually come to light.
18. You are considered near perfect in looks.
19. Somewhat thoughtless but good at heart.
20. Yes, and you will live happily ever after.
21. There is certainly danger in it but, if you are careful, there is no real reason why you should not.
22. This very day.
23. Not before you have written one.
24. The first to confess love for you.
25. Yes, from someone you can't stand.
26. You will certainly have the opportunity.
27. Not for a very long time.
28. Yes, but it will break someone's heart.
29. Writing a letter, but not to you.
30. A wealthy person.
31. Yes.

32. This very day.

NINE

1. You are in their thoughts by day and dreams by night.
2. Not for a very long time.
3. Be gentle and patient and do not contradict.
4. It's now immaterial—tears will flow whether you do or not.
5. If you do you will later regret it.
6. One tall, slender, handsome person with dark eyes.
7. Once, to a real tyrant.
8. Congenial but apt to over-eat.
9. That you are still quite childish in many ways.
10. You would deeply hurt her/him if you didn't.
11. You cannot imagine just how much.
12. Yes . . . you along with all the rest!
13. You will fall in love very soon, after some unhappiness.
14. Within six years.
15. Yes, many.
16. Not very.
17. Not for a while.
18. Your face is considered your greatest asset.
19. Possibly.
20. If it were not for a very bitter enemy of his.
21. If you do, there will be many tears . . . both of sorrow and of joy.
22. Only if you make the first move.

23. No, the people you want to hear from are all preoccupied.
24. The one who will stumble when next with you.
25. Yes, but an insignificant one.
26. You will certainly not want for invitations.
27. Not in any matter of importance.
28. Yes, but it will make many enemies.
29. Buying new clothes.
30. A military person.
31. No.
32. Tomorrow possibly, if not then by next week.

TEN

1. Yes, and affectionately.
2. Why do you ask? They are already on their knees before you!
3. Try not to make a joke out of everything. Some things need to be treated seriously.
4. Reflect on what that might lead to.
5. Do so as though it's unimportant and you'll come to no harm.
6. At least three.
7. One short, one tall, and one medium height.
8. Short and with a large nose.
9. You were always thought to be an angel but now it appears there's a bit of the devil in you.
10. Try for as long as you honestly feel you can.
11. Without you all would be darkness.
12. Yes, but it is thought that you also love others.

13. Very soon you will fall in love with someone you thought you couldn't stand.
14. Not for seven years.
15. Many, and when you least expect to.
16. For a short time, but your foolishness will impoverish you.
17. No.
18. At times, with certain expressions, you are captivating.
19. No one would dispute it.
20. Yes, but you won't be as happy as you thought possible.
21. It really doesn't matter one way or the other.
22. There has been a misunderstanding that will take time to heal.
23. Very soon. A very nice letter.
24. The stoutest.
25. Not for some time.
26. A very long one.
27. When you decide it should be.
28. Yes, but it will cause envy and that will bring you sorrow.
29. Making plans that do not include you.
30. Someone connected with the sea.
31. A blessing to you and a delight to your friends.
32. Not the wished for, but very different news.

TEN

1. Not yet.
2. Someone desperately wants to, and hopes to.

3. Whatever you do, you won't be able to do enough.
4. Meditate on whether it would be right.
5. If it will give you pleasure, yes.
6. Three, one whose name starts with a "W."
7. Once, to someone you already know, whose name starts with a "J."
8. A very funny person, full of tricks and jokes.
9. "If I only knew what to do to gain favor."
10. Test carefully first before trusting fully.
11. In secret, but may never say so out loud.
12. Yes, but is afraid you may not.
13. It's not free at the moment, but will be free again very soon.
14. This year.
15. One big one very soon.
16. Yes, but you must handle money carefully or you will lose it.
17. Very soon.
18. You look better in the evening than you do earlier in the day.
19. You can sometimes be very silly but people generally overlook that, knowing you will grow out of it.
20. No, for they will never marry.
21. Do it, and enjoy it!
22. It's possible that you may never meet again.
23. In a few days.
24. The one who laughs most easily.
25. Possibly tomorrow, though there may be a delay.
26. Yes, across the ocean.

7. Somewhat, and agreeably.
8. That will depend on your behavior.
9. Thinking of you and longing to be with you.
10. A medical person.
11. It will, at least, cause you many happy hours.
12. Unless you work towards it, no, never.

ELEVEN

1. Yes, but with some bitterness.
2. Someone you will meet within the next three days.
3. Whatever you like, for there's really no pleasing them.
4. At least wait for a letter to arrive before answering.
5. If you do, the person who asked will then laugh at you.
6. Two; one distantly related.
7. Once, to the person you now consider the least likely.
8. A good-for-nothing who will bring you nothing but trouble.
9. That you are an enigma.
10. Not too much. Be cautious.
11. Truly and faithfully.
12. S/he is too jealous to be certain.
13. No, it will shortly be stolen.
14. Before next winter.
15. Not soon, but in due course.
16. You could become so if you put your mind to it.

17. You have nothing to fear.
18. Only by your lover.
19. Your heart is pure and your mind is clear.
20. Of course!
21. Consider first whether or not anyone would get harmed.
22. Yes, very unexpectedly.
23. Tomorrow.
24. The one with the snub nose.
25. Yes, very soon.
26. A delightful journey westward.
27. Not as soon as you expect nor in the way you expect.
28. If you really wish it, yes.
29. Reading one of your letters.
30. A tradesperson.
31. It is extremely doubtful.
32. Very soon, but all your expectations will not be gratified.

TWELVE

1. Yes, though s/he is afraid of getting carried away with such thoughts.
2. An older person.
3. Let your love see that you return their love.
4. Yes, but in a cheerful, laughing way.
5. It will be a step with important consequences.
6. Many, but none of them serious.
7. However many times, it would be better if it were none.

8. Handsome and brilliant. You will be made for each other.
9. That you are overly sentimental.
10. Who else if not?
11. As much as you love her/him.
12. S/he thinks it's impossible, yet hopes it's so.
13. Not for more than a year.
14. When cats lay eggs!
15. You are too cautious.
16. You will always have as much as you have at present.
17. There is someone amongst your friends who will betray you.
18. As a beautiful flower.
19. You are thought to be thoughtless.
20. Don't let go. In the end there will be surrender.
21. If you can without being embarrassed.
22. Before the spring.
23. In a few weeks, a long one.
24. The one you met by chance.
25. Someone is considering giving you one, but is undecided.
26. Yes, to Europe.
27. Very soon and drastically.
28. Not entirely.
29. Longing to be with you.
30. An artist.
31. Decidedly. You will be very happy because of it.
32. The tidings are close at hand and will be more agreeable than you could hope.

Front of a Bow-Top Vardo

DOMINOES

Somewhat akin to dice are dominoes. Many Gypsy *vardos* hold a set of dominoes. It's a good game for passing the time, and also a means of earning money by dukkerin' with them. There are at least two ways of working with them.

Past/Present/Future

One thing that makes dominoes unique for fortunetelling is that, in this method at least, two or three people can have their fortune told at the same time.

The dominoes are spread out over the table, face down, and generally mixed. Up to three people may then draw off three dominoes each. They draw them with their left hand and place them, still face down, in a line horizontally across in front of them. Turning them over, they are interpreted as follows:

The domino on the Querent's left represents the past; that in the middle, the present; that on the right, the future.

Sixes: all sixes are connected, in a general way,

with good luck.

Fives: all fives refer to jobs and careers.

Fours: all fours deal with money matters.

Threes: all threes are to do with love and love affairs.

Twos: all twos refer to close friends and family.

Ones: all ones refer to journeys and travel.

Blanks: all blanks refer directly to the Querent.

From these general meanings it is easy to give a quick reading of the upturned dominoes. For example: suppose the first domino is a Two/Three, the second is a One/Five and the third a Four/Blank. You would say that in the past (first domino) the client had a lot of very close family and friends with much love all around. At present (second one) she is having to do a lot of traveling in connection with her job. And in the future (third) is going to have to give serious consideration to finances as they affect the querent personally.

In addition to these simple meanings, however, there are some special "double" combinations that must be considered:

Double-Six: The marriage of the querent. If already married, then good fortune coming as the result of a wedding.

Double-Five: A promotion at work, to a higher and better paid position.

Double-Four: Unexpected money coming in a dramatic way.

Double-Three: The querent will be falling in love unexpectedly.

Double-Two: Development of new friends who will become very close and dear.

Double-One: A wonderful vacation journey that will be thoroughly enjoyable.

Double-Blank: This is one domino that is considered very unlucky. The querent should exercise exteme caution in all things.

The Seven Veils

This is a reading done for a single querent, using all the dominoes. Again they are laid out, face down, and "shuffled" by the client. One domino is drawn, turned up and interpreted, then returned to the set face down again. They are once more shuffled and a second domino is chosen. This is interpreted and returned, face down. For a third time they are mixed, and one is picked and read. This is done up for a total of seven times. But it doesn't have to be seven; it could be only six, four, one, or any number less than seven that is chosen and read. It may not be *more* than seven, however. If the same domino is drawn more than once, it is an indication that the forces at work are very strong and the event will happen very soon.

In this form of reading here are individual meanings given to each domino:

Double-Blank: A dull life; can also be an indication of loss and unhappiness.

One-Blank: Encounter with a stranger who will cause some unhappiness.

Two-Blank: The start of a new partnership, but it will lead nowhere, or to unhappiness.

Three-Blank: Problems brought about by jealousy and/or wrong decisions.

Four-Blank: You will receive a letter bearing bad news.

Five-Blank: You will attend a funeral, though not of a relative.

Six-Blank: Guard yourself against scandal. Possibility of scandal spread by someone you thought to be a friend.

Double-One: Now is the time to make a bold decision; things are perfectly in balance.

Two-one: You will lose money or property in the near future.

Three-One: An unexpected discovery; a pleasant surprise.

Four-One: Time to pay your debts if you are to stay out of trouble.

Five-One: The chance for a passionate, romantic love affair.

Six-One: Decision time ... this could be the start or end of all you have dreamed of.

Double-Two: Both your home life and your business life are on solid ground. Beware of upsetting either boat.

Three-Two: Avoid taking any chances, especially gambling. You would be the loser.

Four-Two: Your investments, both in business and in life/love, will double.

Five-Two: Increase ... profits in business or a child born.

Six-Two: You will receive a gift that will be extremely useful to you.

Double-Three: The marriage of an ex-love will aggravate you.

Four-Three: You will meet an ex-love you had all but forgotten.

Five-Three: A promotion.

Six-Three: You will be invited to a party. If you go you will thoroughly enjoy it.

Double-Four: You will be invited to a party. If you go you will thoroughly enjoy it.

Five-Four: A gamble pays off, but don't push your luck.

Six-Four: You will be involved in a lawsuit. Be cautious.

Double-Five: Relocation, to your great advantage.

Six-Five: You are in a position to help others. It would be good to do so.

Double-Six: Success in all things.

A "Ledge" style caravan (one of the best publicly-owned examples) manufactured by **Dunton & Sons, of Reading, Berkshire, England. Originally owned by the Buckland family and now in the Kentwood House Museum, Hampstead Heath, London. (circa 1905)**

—Photo courtesy of English Heritage (The Iveagh Bequest, Kentwood, London)

MOLES

Gypsies are very superstitious when it comes to moles on the body. It is thought that they are very positive indications of character and of events to come.

The larger the mole, the greater the prosperity or adversity that will come. If the mole is round, it signifies good; if oblong, a moderate share of good fortune; if angular, a fair mix of good and bad. The deeper the color of the mole, the more pronounced the effect, be it good or bad.

Moles on different parts of the body have different meanings, as follows:

Forehead: If a mole is in the center of the forehead, it predicts an active, industrious disposition with success in business and a happy marriage. But if the mole is on the side of the forehead, it's not so favorable, particularly on the left side. On the right side, or temple, it shows an industrious disposition with an interest in love and lovemaking; a great success in life generally, with a much-loved marriage partner.

167

On the left side, much the same but far harder work will be needed in all areas to achieve the same success.

Eyebrows: A mole on the right eyebrow signifies a sprightly, active disposition; courage and perseverance. There will be wealth and success in love, business and war. You will marry an agreeable mate and live happily, with many children. On the left eyebrow it shows an indolent, peevish temper; a leaning towards alcohol, cowardice, and little interest in love *per se*. You will experience many disappointments in life and have no children.

Eyes: A mole on the outside corner of either eye shows a sober, honest and steady disposition, much inclined to the pleasures of love. It also foretells a violent death after a life of ups and downs.

Nose: Moles on any part of the nose show a hasty and passionate disposition, much given to amorous pursuits. You are faithful, open and sincere in your friendships. Tend to be petulant and tempted by alcohol. You will be successful throughout life and will "marry well," if not necessarily happily.

Cheek: On either cheek, a mole shows an industrious, benevolent person. Little inclined to athletic sports, yet very courageous. You will become neither rich nor very poor, but will be better off than your parents were.

Ear: On either ear a mole denotes riches. If on the lower tip of the ear, stay away from water; there is a chance of drowning.

Lips: A mole on either lip shows a delicate person who must watch their diet and curb their appetite.

Their health will always need attention.

Chin: An amiable and quiet disposition. Very agreeable and friendly. Industrious and with a love of travel. Highly successful in business. A good partner, in business or life.

Neck: In front of the neck is a good sign; on the back of the neck is misfortune. On either side it foretells that you will become quarrelsome and devious as you grow older.

Shoulder: On the left shoulder, a person who is quarrelsome and inclined to dispute anything and everything. It indicates a life that varies little almost to the point of monotony. There will be many children and moderate success in business. On the right shoulder it shows a person who is prudent and discreet, one with much wisdom and great tact and diplomacy. Very industrious but not too amorous. Would make a very good partner in anything.

Armpit: You are very good looking and will become rich and benevolent.

Arm: On either arm it indicates a courteous disposition, together with fortitude, resolution, and fidelity. In men it also indicates that he will fight many battles and be successful in them all. It also shows a leaning to generosity and prosperity.

Elbow: A mole on either elbow shows a restless and unsteady disposition with a great desire to travel. Discontent with marriage; no great interest in amassing personal possessions. Friendly and faithful in friendship.

Wrist: You are ingenious; an inventor; an "idea" person.

Hand: Moles on either hand, so long as they are not on the fingers, denote wealth, industry and energy generally, in either sex.

Fingers: On any finger it is an indication that you will be a thief and never be wealthy.

Back: If below the shoulder blades, you will have a hard life, with many disappointments. If above the shoulder blades, you will face many challenges but rise to defeat them.

Buttocks: Signifies shiftlessness and probable poverty. You will tend to be lazy.

Chest: A quarrelsome and unhappy temper. You are extremely amorous and can become uncontrollable.

Breasts: A mole on the right breast shows you are given to drink and can become overly amorous. You will have many sudden reversals in your fortunes. Beware of pretended friends. A mole on the left breast shows that you are industrious and of sober disposition. Slow to arouse, but can be a good lover. You will have much success in life and many children.

Nipple: In a woman it is a sign that she will have a child who will become famous. In a man it denotes that he will be fond of women and spend too much time pursuing them.

Side: On either side, near the ribs, shows a cowardly disposition. You are given to excess in all things. You will have a relatively easy life, though not a luxurious one.

Hip: A mole on either hip shows a contented disposition. You are industrious, amorous, and very faithful to family and friends. You will have moderate success in life. All you receive you will have earned.

Navel: On a woman it denotes many children and a good marriage. On a man it is a sign that he will be lucky in all he undertakes, will become rich and will have a son who will be distinguished.

Stomach: If in the pit of the stomach it shows a person who is somewhat foppish, with little common sense. It also denotes riches. If lower on the stomach, it's a sign that you will promise more than you will perform but will, nevertheless, be held in high esteem.

Genitals: A generous, honest and open disposition. Well mannered and gallant. A lover of love (rather than of sex) though not to excess. You will have a very happy marriage and, although you may not become rich, you will never want for anything. A woman with a mole on the *mons* will become the mother of a great genius.

Groin: On the right groin denotes riches and honors, but to be accompanied by disease. On the left groin you will have the sickness without the wealth.

Thigh: On the right thigh it shows a person with an agreeable temper, inclined to be amorous, and very courageous. On the left thigh it shows a person who is good and benevolent, hard working, and with no great interest in the pleasures of love-making.

Knee: On the left knee it shows a hasty and passionate disposition, extravagance, no great leaning towards hard work nor honesty. On the right knee it indicates an amiable temper, honest disposition, great success in love, and many good friends.

Leg: Moles on either leg show a person who is thoughtless, and given to extravagance. There will be many difficulties throughout life, usually brought about by your own actions. In general you will have more fortune than misfortune, but you will tend to remember, and dwell upon, the bad more than the good.

Ankle: Effeminacy in men, with a certain amount of cowardice. However, in women it is a sign of courage.

Foot: A mole on either foot shows a melancholy disposition. Very inactive. Little inclined to do anything, not even follow the desires of your heart. Moles on the feet frequently foretell sickness and unexpected misfortune, with much sorrow.

Heel: A spiteful and malevolent disposition, but a person full of energy.

Instep: You will be quarrelsome and have few friends. You will be a great walker.

Toes: You will marry someone rich but be very unhappy.

FIRE READING

The *Rom* spend many long hours sitting around the *yag* at the *atchen' tan*—the campfire. It's hardly surprising, then, that they can use that fire for divining. Gazing through half-closed eyes, seemingly dreamily, into the glowing embers, they are frequently able to make contact with . . . what? Their inner sight? The universal unconscious? Race memories? To connect up with others' thoughts, in what is generally termed Extra Sensory Perception? Whatever the label you care to use, the Gypsies themselves don't attempt to explain it. As with so many things, they just accept it as part of their natural selves.

Any number of people can read their own fortunes in the same fire, for the formations of the embers appear differently to each person, and are also interpreted by that person in their own individual way. This is the sort of divination that, although someone else can do it for you, it's probably far better you do for yourself.

If you *are* doing it for someone else (a client), then sit with that person on your left; their right hand held between your own two hands as you gaze into the fire. Spend a few moments attuning to that person before focusing your gaze into the fire itself.

It may be that, no matter how long you gaze into the fire, you can see nothing that seems to have any real meaning to you. This is not necessarily an unfavorable sign but simply means that the forces at work are presently changing rapidly and have not settled into any sort of a complete picture. Give up and try again the next night, when they may have stabilized. Don't fire-gaze for longer than ten minutes at any one time.

Interpretation

How to interpret what you see? You can do no better than to follow the advice I gave for teacup reading.

You represent the client, so those symbols closest to you (as with the handle of the teacup) will be the ones which most affect the client.

Time is judged by position: any symbol near the top of the fire is in the present; the lower down the fire it appears, the further into the future it will be.

Those symbols on the left of the fire are more likely to be negative symbols, while those on the right are more likely to be positive.

Also as in tea leaf reading, the way a symbol faces may well have a specific meaning, particularly as to positive or negative influence.

To reiterate what I said above: don't expect all

the symbols to look exactly like the things they represent. You will have to use your imagination a great deal. You will find that there is usually just a suggestion of, say, a bird or a rabbit or whatever. These suggestions are enough to trigger your mind into seeing them. Use the symbols simply as a focal point and go with your psychic feelings. Review all the meanings I gave for tea leaf reading and apply those to the images in the fire.

One final tip. If the fire has died down a lot and you find that the embers are getting very dull, simply throw a handful of salt onto the fire. It will cause it to flare up again long enough for you to complete your reading.

Ray Buckland and Peter Ingram, a Gypsy who restores old Gyspy wagons, in front of a beautiful Bow-Top Ingram has restored.

CRYSTALS
AND GEMSTONES

In the popular mind, Gypsies wear a great deal of gold and silver; bracelets and necklaces, gold coins (especially as decoration on clothing), many silver and gold rings on the fingers. This isn't an incorrect picture, certainly of Gypsies in the past, but the reason for it is not ostentation. These days the Rom are perhaps not quite so obvious, but still do keep their money to themselves. The reason is simply that they do not trust the *gaujo's* banks. That and the fact that in the days before twenty-four hour money machines, and chains of banks across the country, they never knew when they would be anywhere near a bank. It was therefore much more convenient (and, to their eyes, safer) to keep their money about their person. Not only do they keep their wealth in coin, but also in jewels.

There is a tremendous interest today in crystals, precious and semi-precious stones. Gypsies have always been aware of their occult significance. They wear them and carry them and use them, not as followers of a current fad but as keepers of the

Romani Mysteries. A future book in this Romani series of mine will deal exclusively with the subject. Here, however, I will simply detail how such stones are used by them for divination.

First let's look at popular beliefs in the properties of the major stones, together with their meanings when used for Romani divination.

Agate: Also known as "Scotch Pebble." This is a semi-precious stone with bands of color, usually brown, dark red or yellow, or sometimes blue or green. It's associated with people born in the astrological sign of Gemini. An old rhyme goes as follows:

Who comes with the summer to this earth,
And owes to June her hour of birth,
With ring of agate on her hand
Can wealth, health and long life command.

Agate is supposed to be especially lucky for farmers, foresters, gardners and all connected with the land. It gives strength to the heart and will cure snake bites.

For Romani divination, agate represents a pleasant surprise.

Amethyst: A variety of quartz, with purple, violet or mauve coloring. It is associated with Aquarians. The old rhyme is:

The February born shall find
Sincerity and peace of mind,
Freedom from passion and from care,
If they the amethyst will wear.

The stone is most popularly associated with drunkenness. If an amethyst is placed in a glass of water and allowed to steep there, the water can later be drunk and will cure the drunkenness. The stone is also lucky for lovers and brings faithfulness in love to those who wear it, also freedom from jealousy and anger. Additionally it is good for counteracting magickal charms.

The Romani divination meaning is that you will lose something of value.

Bloodstone: A semi-precious stone which is dark green with red spots that look like small bloodstains. It was thought that it had the power to stop bleeding. Associated with those born under the sign of Pisces, the rhyme goes:

Who on this world of ours their eyes
In March first open, shall be wise,
In days of peril strong and brave,
And wear a bloodstone to their grave.

Many soldiers used to carry such a stone into battle with them. It was said to ward off illness and give courage to its wearer.

The Romani meaning, for divination, is that there will be an unpleasant surprise coming.

Diamond: A pure form of carbon, usually crystal clear and very sparkling. It is said to be luckiest when worn on the left side. Associated with Aries, the rhyme is:

She who from April dates her years,
Diamonds shall wear, lest bitter tears
For vain repentance flow. This stone
Emblem of innocence is known.

Vest of a Gypsy "Dukkerer"

It symbolizes strength, virtue and bravery, also insight. Worn around the neck it ensures safe childbirth. Gypsies believe that it will lose its sparkle if touched by the hand of a traitor.

The divinatory meaning is of a business advancement.

Emerald: A precious stone of the beryl type, but distinguished from beryl by its beautiful green color. Associated with Taurus, the rhyme is:

Who first beholds the light of day
In spring's sweet, flowery month of May,
And wears an emerald all her life.
Shall be a loved and loving wife.

The emerald was supposed to be good for eyesight and also to strengthen memory. Romani lore says that if given by one lover to another, it will pale and grow dull if love should fade between them.

Its meaning in divination is a secret admirer.

Garnet: A semi-precious stone, usually red or reddish brown, sometimes yellow, black or green. It brings a healthy and cheerful disposition and is associated with the sign of Capricorn.

By her who in this month was born
No gem save garnets shall be worn.
They will ensure her constancy,
True friendship and fidelity.

Garnets are also believed to ward off inflammatory diseases.

Divination meaning is that you will receive a letter.

Opal: A precious stone of cloudy white, but flashing with rainbow hues as it catches the light. For the Libra.

> October's child is born for woe,
> And life's vicissitudes must know;
> But lay an opal on her breast,
> And hope will lull those woes to rest.

For other than the Libran it is considered an unlucky stone to wear in an engagement ring. The Gypsies say that for anyone else the marriage will never take place. For those whose birthstone it is, however, it will give the power of second sight. As with the emerald, it will lose its brilliance if worn by an unfaithful lover.

Romani divination meaning is of death—not necessarily to the querent but certainly to someone close to them.

Ruby: Considered by many the most precious of all jewels. Except for the color, it is the same in composition as sapphire, with similar brilliance. It is usually thought of as being a glowing red but it may range between pink and almost violet. The jewel for Cancer, the rhyme is:

> The glowing ruby shall adorn
> Those who in warm July are born.
> Then will they be exempt and free
> From love's doubt and anxiety.

The ruby is good for cases of poisoning (used as was the amethyst for drunkenness). It gets rid of depression and all evil thoughts. It brings good fortune and friendship.

In divination, the ruby indicates the influence of a stranger.

Sapphire: A precious stone which is usually a clear cornflower blue. The stone of Virgo:

> A maiden born when autumn leaves
> Are rustling in September's breeze,
> A sapphire on her brow should bind;
> 'Twill cure diseases of the mind.

This gem is lucky for lovers and brings peaceful, optimistic happiness. It is good for inflammation of the eyes and generally attracts good fortune.

Meaning in Romani divination is that a wrong done in the past will catch up with the querent.

Sardonyx: A variety of onyx which has white and dark red or white and dark brown markings in bands or layers. It is associated with Leo.

> Wear a sardonyx or for thee
> No conjugal felicity.
> The August-born without this stone,
> 'Tis said, must live unloved alone.

Protecting against the bite of snakes, the sardonyx also brings happiness to married couples.

The divinatory meaning is that there will be a wedding in the future, though not necessarily of the querent her/himself.

Topaz: A more or less transparent precious stone which is usually clear yellow but sometimes yellowish white, blue or even pink. The stone of Scorpio, the rhyme says:

Who first comes to this world below
In drear November's fog and snow,
Should prize the topaz' amber hue,
Emblem of friends and lovers true.

Gypsies consider it good for warding off chest complaints, rheumatic troubles and asthma. It is also considered to bring fidelity in love and friendship.

The meaning in divination is that caution needs to be exercised.

Turquoise: A translucent or opaque precious stone of a blue or blue-green color. Its coloring and luster vary with the feelings of the wearer. Associated with Sagittarius, the old rhyme goes:

If cold December gave you birth,
The month of snow and ice and mirth,
Place on your hand a turquoise blue,
Success will bless whate'er you do.

The stone protects from danger and misfortune. When the wearer is near death, the stone will fade to a very pale shade.

In divination, it is the sign of an imminent journey.

These twelve are the stones most generally used for divination; these or suitable substitutes (e.g. clear quartz for diamond; amber for topaz). A circle of roughly eighteen inches in diameter is drawn on the ground, or table. A rough stone is taken from the ground in the vicinity of where the divination is being done. This is placed with the other stones and will serve as the Significator. The querent will then take all thirteen stones in his/her hands, shake them together, and throw them into the circle. If the Significator stone rolls outside the circle, s/he must throw them again. If it rolls out a second time, no fortune can be told for twenty-four hours.

The stones are read according to their relationship to one another and to the Significator. Whether or not the stones are interpreted as Sun signs or purely according to their divinatory meanings seems up to the feelings of the dukkerer. For example, supposing that the Significator falls next to the ruby and close to the topaz. The diviner might say that you should exercise caution (topaz) when a stranger tries to influence you (ruby), or she might say that you should be cautious should you come into contact with a person born under the sign of Cancer (of course it may well be that the stranger is a Cancer!).

The stones need to be studied according to how they fall, and their relationship to one another. Positioning within the circle has bearing on the time frame. The closer to the center of the circle, the closer to the present. The closer to the edge of the circle, the further into the future.

Some Gypsies do not use the Significator stone. They draw two lines across the circle, at approximately one-third intervals, and take the closest area as the present, the center section as the near future (within about six months) and the furthest section as the far distant future. Relative position to the center line indicates relative influence on the querent.

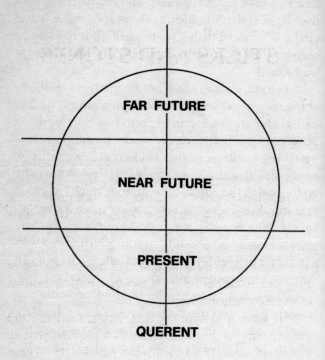

Gemstone Layout for Divination

STICKS AND STONES

Kosh, or *kosht*, is the Romanes for "stick," and *bar* is the word for "stone." *Dukkerin' kosht* is therefore the true name for divining with sticks, and *dukkerin' bars* for divining with stones.

I have seen many Gypsies in the southwest of England dukkerin' kosht; it seems to be little known in the north, however,
  [I gave a version of this, based on the Rom variety, in my books *Buckland's Complete Book of Witchcraft*, and *The Tree*. There I called it "Saxon Wands"]
  Seven sticks are needed for this. They are usually cut from the hedgerow and are nothing special other than being more or less straight. Four of the sticks should be longer than the other three. I'd suggest the three at about nine inches in length and the four at about twelve inches. One of the twelve-inch ones should be much thicker than the others. This one is referred to as the *kralisi* ("Queen").
  To use them, you lay the *kralisi* on the ground

horizontally in front of you. Take the other six *koshes* and hold them out over the *kralisi*. Close your eyes and concentrate on the question you need answered. Rub your hands together to mix up the sticks. Keeping your eyes closed, grip all the sticks in your right hand and then take hold of the tip of one of them with your left hand. Open your right hand and let the sticks fall, except for the one your left hand is holding.

You will see—on opening your eyes—that the five sticks have fallen on or over the *kralisi*. Here is how you interpret the way they have fallen:

a. If there are more of the *longer* sticks than the shorter ones on the ground, then the answer is in the affirmative.

b. If there are more of the *shorter* ones than the longer ones (excluding the *kralisi*), then the answer is in the negative.

c. If any koshes actually *touch* the *kralisi*, it indicates that the answer will be a very positive one, or will take place in a very positive way, with strong forces at work.

d. If any koshes are *off the ground*, resting on others, then regardless of *a* or *b* no definite answer can be given at this time, for things are still "up in the air."

e. If all the sticks point *toward* the *kralisi*, then the querent will have a very definite part to play in the determination of the question.

f. If *none* of the koshes point *toward* the *kralisi*, then the matter will be determined with no involvement on the part of the querent.

This is a simple, yet effective, method of getting an answer to a quesstion. By choosing your ques on(s) carefully, you can often narrow a problem own till you've completely solved it. As with all omani divination, it is of an extremely practical ature, using the simplest of tools yet providing ositive answers.

Dukkerin' bars are used a great deal for getting Yes/No" answers to questions. It is similar, in this espect, to the use of the pendulum (see *Needles*, elow) but is much easier.

A Gypsy will pick up two small round stones they don't have to be found at the same time. In fact 's not uncommon to search for a very long time efore finding the two that seem "just right" for the ndividual), somewhere between the size of an acorn nd a walnut. One should be white, or light, in color nd the other black, or dark, and they should both e of approximately the same shape and size. These re carefully washed and from then on usually carried n a little bag hung from the belt or on a thong round the neck.

To use the stones, they are simply cupped in he hands and shaken like dice, while the question o be answered is concentrated on. They are then hrown down. If they land with the white stone loser to the thrower than the dark stone, then the nswer is in the positive. If they land with the dark tone closer, then the answer is in the negative. If hey land side by side, equidistant, then the question nust be asked again or rephrased. The dukkerin' ars are as simple as that.

Interior of a Gypsy "Vardo"
(Wagon or Caravan)

KNIVES AND NEEDLES

There are two very simple forms of divining that are used a lot by Gypsy children (*chavvies*), as well as by their elders. At first glance they may seem little more than parlor games, yet they can provide answers to questions as well as many far more complicated methods. The first of these is by spinning a knife.

Amongst their kitchen utensils, many Gypsy vardos include a round wooden bread board, about twelve inches in diameter. These are most commonly used for the knife divination. A round salver, or similar, will do just as well. If nothing else, then cut out a circle from a sheet of cardboard.

A regular kitchen knife is used and is placed in the center of the board. Around the edges of the board are placed pieces of paper (about two inches long by an inch or so wide) on which have been written suitable "answers." Some of the most commonly used ones are:

Yes.

No.

You must have patience.
Beware of false friends.
Good news is coming.
A letter is expected.
Success in business.
An unexpected visitor.
Love is here.
Tears will turn to joy.
News from abroad.
A new admirer.
An unexpected meeting.
A journey.
An important letter.

The question is concentrated upon, then the querent spins the knife by its center. It is twirled three times in all, giving three messages. Of these, one (though not necessarily the first received) will be an answer to the original question, while the other two will be further messages which may or may not be related to it.

Should the knife stop equidistant between two of the messages, then that spin can be discounted and the knife spun again.

Divining with needles is very simple indeed. Twenty-one new needles are placed in a saucer or plate. Water is then slowly poured in on them. However gently the water is poured, it will be found that the needles move. The Gypsies say that as many needles as cross each other indicate the number of enemies, or forces working against you, that you will encounter that month (moon's period).

A needle may also be used as a pendulum. The needle is threaded with red silk thread (approximately nine inches long). The end of the thread is then held, with the needle hanging down, and questions are asked.

The client is asked for a coin (a silver coin was traditional . . . a quarter will do!). This is placed on the table and you sit with the end of the thread in your hand, elbow resting on the table, and the needle suspended just above the coin. The client may ask as many questions as s/he wishes, though they should be questions that can be answered "Yes" or "No" only. You should try to keep your hand quite still, yet you will find that as you concentrate on the question, the needle will start to swing.

A swing backwards and forwards, towards you and away from you, indicates "Yes." A swing across you indicates "No." If the needle simply swings around in a circle, it means that the question is vague; it needs to be rephrased. If it hangs without swinging, then the question cannot be answered at this time.

For more sophisticated methods of using a pendulum, please see my book *Practical Color Magick* (Llewellyn, 1983).

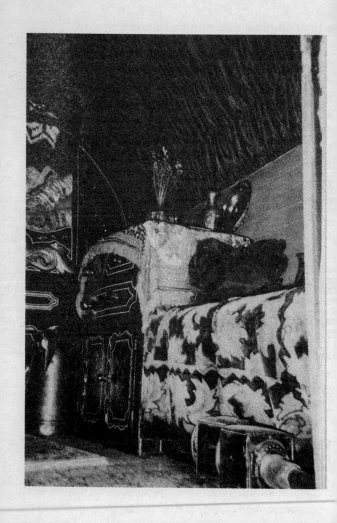

Interior of a Bow-Top Vardo

OMENS AND PORTENTS
Bok and *Kushti Bok*

Bok is bad luck, and *kushti bok* is good luck.

I will give some of the major omens regarded by the Romani in England. It would take a huge book to contain all the many little signs and circumstances. I am certainly not going to deal here with such things as spilling salt, breaking mirrors and walking under ladders. That is not to say that there is not "something to them," it is just that they have been dealt with adequately in just about every book written that deals with superstitions.

Of the following, don't be too quick to laugh at some of these beliefs. They are usually held after many generations' observance, and are extremely valid; if not true one hundred per cent of the time, certainly a very high percentage.

It is considered an ill omen to see a spider early in the morning. The earlier in the morning, and the larger the spider, the greater the evil that threatens you. But it is only if the spider is indoors—and especially if in your bedroom—that it is so significant.

Outdoors it bodes no harm. Gypsies also say that this refers basically to the house spider. The wood spider is not to be dreaded. In fact, do not on any account kill a wood spider or you will draw to you the hatred of the whole race of spiders and, sooner or later, would suffer by it.

When found in the evening, a spider signifies good luck. A Rom saying goes: *"Sarla, tugno. Rarti, doodani"*—literally, "Morning, sadness. Evening, shining" (or "hope"). The smaller the spider; the greater the good fortune. Tiny spiders have much less bad luck in them than the larger ones. Daddy longlegs are always messengers of *good* luck.

From time immemorial, the horseshoe has been considered a sign of luck. It is a blending of two elements—the shape of the shoe (that of a crescent moon) and the metal of the shoe (iron). As Dr. G. Storms points out (in *Anglo-Saxon Magic*), for millennia iron has been considered magical, partly from the mysterious way in which it was originally found, in meteoric stones. Gypsies have an especial regard for horses. In fact, it is not the dog but the horse that is considered the Gypsy's best friend. With all these elements, then, it is hardly surprising that the Rom consider the horseshoe a symbol for luck. Many a vardo will have a horseshoe hung over the entrance . . . hung with the points up, to hold in the luck. Incidentally, Nelson, the great English admiral, had such faith in the horseshoe that he always had one nailed to the main mast of his ship *Victory*.

If a Gypsy finds a horseshoe lying in the road with the points toward him, he will spit on it and throw it over his left shoulder. This is to counteract any bad luck that was held in the shoe and has now come from it to him.

If a horse rolls on the ground, rolling over and back again, then this is a sign of good fortune coming, usually connected with money. To meet a red-headed person riding a white horse is extremely good luck.

In the north of England—good horse country—the Rom say that if a horse runs around neighing loudly, someone nearby is dying.

If your right ear tingles, or itches, someone is speaking well of you. If your left ear tingles, they are speaking ill of you. To find out who it is, call out loud the names of all those you think it could be. The tingling will stop when you call out the correct name.

If your nose itches early in the morning, you will receive good news later in the day. Gypsies in the west of England say that the itching nose means that you will have company come to visit that day. A nosebleed is an omen of bad luck.

To accidentally put your left shoe on your right foot is a sure sign of an accident to come. Scott, in his *Discovery of Witchcraft*, says: "He that receiveth a mischance will consider whether he put not on his shirt wrong side outwards, or his left shoe on his right foot." Gypsies are not concerned about putting on their shirts inside out, but they do take note of the wrong shoe.

To have a picture drop out of its frame, or to have a stone fall out of its setting, is a very bad omen. If the picture is that of a relative, it could mean the coming death of that relative. To remove a ring from your finger when you have had it there a number of years is a portent of coming illness.

It is extremely unlucky to kill a ladybug, a swallow, robin or wren. To destroy the nest of one of the birds is equally unlucky. Within the course of a year, the person will break a bone.

If a flock of ducks flies across the road from left to right, it is a fortunate sign; if they fly from right to left, unfortunate. However, if a rabbit runs across your path from left to right, that is unlucky. But you can put matters to rights, apparently, by tearing some article of clothing!

To find a dead crow lying in a road or field is a sign of good luck. But it is extremely unlucky to come across the body of a dead owl.

I have many times seen my grandfather "tickling" trout. He would lay on the riverbank, where the bank overhangs slightly, and let his hand trail down in the water. Apparently trout are fond of lazily floating in the shade provided by the overhanging bank. With his fingers curled up, my grandfather would gently tickle the bellies of the fish, lulling them into some sort of complacency. Then he would slip his fingers around the belly and, in one quick movement, jerk them up out of the water over onto the bank. I have seen him catch a large number of trout this way. But then, in true Gypsy style, he will always leave one of the fish hanging in a tree—to ensure that there will be good fishing there the next time.

It is very unlucky to hear the screech owl at night. This is considered by the Gypsies to be a most unlucky bird. There is an old pastoral poem by Grose that goes:

"Within my cot, where quiet
     gave me rest,
Let the dread screech owl build
     her hated nest.
And from my window o'er the
     country send
Her midnight screams to bode my
     latter end."

Weather Omens

There seem to be more weather omens than there could possibly be changes in the weather! First let's look at omens in the sky itself.

If there is a change from continuing wet and stormy to clear and dry, and that change takes place at the time of either the New or the Full Moon (or close to), then it's likely to remain fine till the next quarter. Similarly, if there is no change in the weather at the quarters, then the existing weather will last for a week or two at least.

If there is a general mist at sunrise, or a "sheep sky" as the Gypsies call it, or white clouds drifting to the northwest, then it will be fine for several days.

If there are many clouds seen in the west at sunrise, and they soon disappear, then there will be fine weather but of short duration.

If there are red clouds in the west at sunset it will be fine; if they have a tint of purple, it will be very fine.

If a layer of fine clouds comes up from the northwest underneath other higher clouds driving more south, then there will be fine weather for a short spell.

If there is lightning without thunder after a clear day, there will be a continuation of fair weather.

If there is a rainbow during wet weather then the rain is passing from us.

If the clouds at sunrise are red then there will be rain within twenty-four hours.

If the sun sets in dark, heavy clouds there will be rain the next day.

If there is a change of wind from west to south, or east to south, then it is going to be wet.

If the lower clouds drive more from the south

than those above, it will be wet.

If the stars above forty-five degrees—especially the North Star—flicker strongly and appear closer than usual, there will be rain.

Let us look at animals and insects and their actions as portents for the weather—something my grandfather was excellent with:

If spiders, in spinning their webs, make the terminating filaments long, the weather will be fine for a number of days (the longer the filaments; the longer will the weather remain fine).

Spiders generally alter their webs every twenty-four hours. If they do so between six and seven o'clock in the evening, it will be a fine night. If they alter their webs in the morning, a fine day. If they work in the rain, you can expect it to clear up and be a nice day. The more active a spider is, the finer the weather will be.

If gnats fly thickly in the setting Sun, expect warm weather. If they are seen a great deal in the spring, expect a warm fall.

If owls screech during foul weather, it will change to fair.

"If a cock crow when he goes to bed,
He will arise with a very wet head."

If sheep and goats spring about and fight more than usual, expect rain. Similarly, if cattle leave off their feeding and chase one another, it is going to rain.

If horses stretch out their necks and sniff the air, and gather together in a corner of the field with their heads turned away from the wind, expect rain. Similarly, if they suddenly stop feeding and begin scratching themselves on trees and fences, there will be heavy rain.

If pigs grow restless and grunt loudly, and if they jerk up their heads, there will be a great deal of wind. If a pig picks up a piece of wood in its mouth it's a sure sign of bad weather. In fact Gypsies have a saying: "Pigs can see the wind."

Other indicators of coming rain are: frogs and toads croaking more than usual; bees remaining in their hives, or only flying a short distance away; worms coming out of the ground in numbers; swallows flying lower than usual; crows making a great deal of noise and flying around in circles; dogs eating grass; cats sneezing and/or washing their face and behind their ears; fish biting more readily and splashing up at the surface of the water.

With flowers, if the marigold stays shut after seven in the evening, it is going to rain. If the convolvulus and chickweed close up, there'll be rain. If the leaves of the trees move without any perceptible breeze, it is going to rain. If oak trees bud earlier than ash trees in the spring, then you can expect a wet summer. If dew lies thickly on the grass after a fair day, it's a sure sign of another fair day coming.

As I have said, there are probably ten or a hundred times as many weather signs as I have given. Different parts of the country seem to favor different signs. The best thing is to study weather changes and keep a log of possible signs, verifying them over long periods. You'll find that soon a definite pattern will emerge.

Gypsy Camp.

COLD READING

What happens when a client comes for a reading and you just aren't "in the mood?" Many Rom have to do readings in order to earn a living. If they are advertising their services and someone comes and pays money, they have to produce. But supposing they can't? Well, then they resort to what is often referred to as a "Cold Reading"—a reading that is not based on any psychic attunement, but is the result of astute observation and deduction; picking up clues from the appearance and reaction of the client. There may be a great deal of psychology involved; but then there generally is in any reading.

For doing a cold reading, some sort of "prop" is a good idea. It serves as a focal point for the client and looks as though the reader really is going from something. The safest, and also the most impressive, is probably a large crystal ball. Too many people have a knowledge of tarot cards these days to be able to use them simply as a prop. You might get away with regular playing cards but, as I say, a crystal is probably the safest and most impressive.

Here are just a few examples of some of the clues that may be picked up from the person who has come for a reading:

When a client loudly boasts about something, he is probably frustrated in some desire(s), and feeling somewhat inferior. A dull, monotonous voice, with slow delivery, shows the client to be feeling defeated; rejected. If he speaks with rising inflection, then he has some doubt about what you have said; he is finding it hard to believe. Short, sharp sentences usually indicate excitement.

To give some generalizations—and that is all they can be—men are generally interested in prestige, be it money, position, or power. Women are frequently jealous, and afraid their husband is being unfaithful. Young people are mostly interested in the opposite sex. Again, these are broad generalizations, and also pretty sexist for today! However, these *are* very pertinent when it comes to *the type of people who frequent Gypsy Dukkerers.* Here are some of the reasons people do go to fortunetellers:

Amusement	Frustration
Curiosity	Wish-fulfillment
Anxiety	Need for a confidant

With this last, many women use a fortuneteller as many men use a bartender—a friendly stranger to whom they can pour out their problems. A great many of life's problems *can* be solved simply by verbalizing them, and certainly by getting unbiased input from another point of view. These are the sort of clients that the Dukkerer loves. No psychic work is actually called for, only good common sense! Just put yourself in the place of the client and decide what *you* would do under the circumstances.

As to anxiety . . . the vast majority of women who have their fortunes told are concerned that someone is "working against them." They believe that someone has placed a curse on them. There are many unscrupulous "Readers" who prey upon these people, encouraging them in this belief and promising to remove the curse—for a fee! Invariably the curse is not removed "because it was stronger than thought," and there is call for a higher fee! This type of "fortuneteller" does dukkerin' a great disservice. Please don't ever resort to what may seem like easy money and play off these poor people.

Continuing with the generalization: the principle problems troubling the female center around love and security. The love here is not just love of the opposite sex, but also love of home, family and friends. The security involves money and love security. Health, too, falls into the love category . . . the health of the woman herself and of her family and loved ones.

Much of this can be obvious to the Romani just be studying the client. For example, when a woman sits twisting her wedding band round and round on her finger, it is a good sign that she has a marriage problem. But frequently the client will burst out with what is worrying her, telling all and just asking advice (or "What do you see for me?").

Let's look at types for a moment. *An attractive young girl* is frequently juggling and judging boy-friends, though it could be that she is unsure of herself and her own attractiveness. Which of these it is, usually becomes quickly apparent.

The plain, homely girl is often afraid of the opposite sex and, indeed, afraid of sex itself. She may be dominated by her mother, or trapped into a stay-at-home life.

An older, unmarried woman (again remembering that we are talking about the type of people who habitually go to fortunetellers) is frequently frustrated and becoming desperate in her search for "Mr. Right." She is frequently lonely and many times bitter. A good clue to this type of woman is her use of sarcasm with regard to anything positive that you might suggest. Sometimes she is suspicious about her "friends"—are they really friends or are they talking behind her back?

Wife and/or mother. Frequently has many worries about whether or not her husband is faithful, about her children (are they into the drug scene?), about money and paying the bills.

The young man is most often troubled about the possible unfaithfulness of his girlfriend. As with the young girl, though, if the young man is a homely type it's more likely that he is troubled by a lack of girlfriends.

Business man. Usually one of two problems (and seldom both together). Either he has a problem in business involving a deal, a promotion, a decision, or he is trying to choose between his wife and his girlfriend.

Elderly people are most often concerned about family members, finances, or what will become of them.

(I cannot stress too strongly—knowing the justifiable sensitivity of many people today, especially women—that these are generalities and that they do *not*, by any means apply to all who fall under these categories. However, what I have listed is true for the vast majority of such people who go looking for advice from a fortuneteller.)

The client has a good idea of what he or she wants to hear, before ever stepping into the Dukkerer's *ofisa*. Always give positive advice, never negative. We do create our own realities, so to put a positive future into the client's mind is to give her the ammunition to bring about what she really desires.

Flatter where possible, without being too obvious.

Here is a list of things you should consider when giving a cold reading:

The physical health of the client.
Their state (e.g. calm; nervous; chain smok-
  ing).
Personality.
Age.
Marital state.
Affluence.

Don't be afraid to ask questions of the client. "Do you have many friends?" is a natural question that may well lead to a whole opening up on the part of the client. "Do you suspect someone of working against you?" is another good one.

It can be useful to know the client's age, yet s/he may be reluctant to divulge it. Here is a handy little device that will determine it for you. It works for anyone aged sixty or under. You make up a set of six cards as shown on pages 211-212.

Giving the cards to the client, ask him to pick out all the cards which contain his age, wherever that happens to be on the card. Take these cards he has picked and quickly, mentally, add together all the numbers in the top right hand corner of each card chosen. The total will be the client's age.

For example, suppose the client's age is 20. He will pick out cards B and E—the only two cards with 20 on them. The top right hand corner numbers are 4 and 16 respectively. Added together, these give the age: 20.

Some dukkerers have a small slip of paper they have the client fill out and sign at the start of the reading. The paper basically says that the client understands that the reading is purely for entertainment purposes. With some of the unfair laws against fortunetelling still used in many states, it is perhaps a good and wise precaution to do this. The clients read it and sign it. Additionally, on this slip of paper, some dukkerers have a line asking for birth month and day (not year, since some people seem sensitive to giving their age). The reason for this added line is that, if you know anything of astrology, by ascertaining the client's birth month and day (you don't need the year, and anyway you can easily determine that from the above cards) you can then apply much of the "typical" Sun sign attributes to your client as part of the cold reading. A knowledge of astrology can certainly stand you in good stead,

CARD A:

3	5	7	9	11	1
13	15	17	19	21	23
25	27	29	31	33	35
37	39	41	43	45	47
49	51	53	55	57	59

CARD B:

5	6	7	13	12	4
14	15	20	21	22	23
28	29	30	31	36	37
52	38	39	44	45	46
47	53	54	55	60	13

CARD C:

9	10	11	12	13	8
14	15	24	25	26	27
28	29	30	31	40	41
42	43	44	45	46	47
56	57	58	59	60	13

CARD D:

3	6	7	10	11	2
14	15	18	19	22	23
26	27	30	31	34	35
38	39	42	43	46	47
50	51	54	55	58	59

CARD E:

17	18	19	20	21	16
22	23	24	25	26	27
28	29	30	31	48	49
50	51	52	53	54	55
56	57	58	59	30	60

CARD F:

33	34	35	36	37	32
38	39	40	41	42	43
44	45	46	47	48	49
50	51	52	53	54	55
56	57	58	59	60	41

where a cold reading is concerned. Incidentally, Gypsies don't generally practice either astrology or numerology (there are exceptions, of course), because they do not care to be bothered with math. They can count and do multiplication and division but they are not generally "into numbers." Hence I have not included either of these forms of divination in this book.

In *Gypsy Sorcery and Fortune Telling* (1891), Charles Godfrey Leland gives some "rules" for cold readings. Not all of them are applicable today, yet many are. They are as follows:

1. It is safe in most cases with middle-aged men to declare that they have had a lawsuit, or a great dispute as to property, which has given them a great deal of trouble. This must be impressively uttered. Emphasis and sinking the voice are of great assistance in fortunetelling. If the subject betrays the least emotion, or admits it, promptly improve the occasion, express sympathy, and "work it up."

2. Declare that a great fortune, or something greatly to the advantage of the subject, or something which will gratify him, will soon come in this way, but that he must be keen to watch his opportunity and be bold and energetic.

3. He will have three great chances, or fortunes, in his life. If you *know* that he has inherited or made a fortune, or had a good appointment, you may say that he has already realized one of them. This seldom fails.

4. A lady of great wealth and beauty, who is of

singularly sympathetic disposition, is in love with him, or ready to be, and it will depend on himself to secure his happiness. Or he will soon meet such a person when he shall least expect it.

5. "You had at one time great trouble with your relations (friends). They treated you very unkindly." Or, "They were prepared to do so but your resolute conduct daunted them."

6. "You have been three times in great danger of death." Pronounce this very impressively. Everybody, though it be a schoolboy, believes or likes to believe that he has encountered perils. This is infallible, or at least it takes in most people. If the subject can be induced to relate his hairbreadth escapes, you may foretell future perils.

7. "You have had an enemy who has caused you great trouble. But he—or she—it is well not to specify which till you find out the sex—will ere long go too far and his or her effort to injure you will recoil on him or her." Or, briefly, "It is written that someone, by trying to wrong you, will incur terrible retribution." Or, "You have had enemies but they are all destined to come to grief." Or, "You had an enemy but you outlived him."

8. "You got yourself once into great trouble by doing a good act."

9. "Your passions have thrice got you into great trouble. Once your inconsiderate anger (or pursuit of pleasure) involved you in great suffering which, in the end, was to your advantage." Or else, "This

will come to pass; therefore be on your guard."

10. "You will soon meet with a person who will have a great influence on your future life if you cultivate his friendship. You will ere long meet someone who will fall in love with you if encouraged."

11. "You will find something very valuable if you keep your eyes open and watch closely. You have twice passed over a treasure and missed it, but you will have a third opportunity."

12. "You have done a great deal of good, or made the fortune or prosperity of persons who have been very ungrateful."

13. "You have been involved in several love affairs, but your conduct in all was really perfectly blameless."

14. "You have great capacity for something, and before long an occasion will present itself for you to exert it to your advantage."

As Leland says, by putting these points carefully, sometimes combining some of them, the fortune-teller can sound amazingly credulous.

A few final points on cold readings.

Remember that human beings like to be flattered. Don't overdo it to become too obvious, but do flatter. Even if the client realizes that you are flattering, he will love you for it!

Speak fairly rapidly. This makes it difficult for the client to remember everything you say and will lead him to think things into the reading that in fact you did not discuss! A vivid imagination and eagerness on the part of the client will cover a lot of ignorance on your part.

Watch the client's reactions carefully. If you get off on the wrong track, it should soon become obvious from these reactions. It can help to periodically say something like, "There are many forces at work at the present time. If I make any important error, as I read, please let me know at once, so that I do not follow a blind path."

Don't hesitate to ask a direct question. The answer can give you important information, which you can enlarge upon as though you had all of it originally.

Don't read for more than one person at a time and don't allow the client to have a friend or friends sitting listening. You don't need an audience . . . or witnesses!

And lastly—*don't do a cold reading unless you absolutely have to.* Far better to do a true reading, using those psychic abilities which we all do possess. Don't forget that the more you use them, the more they will develop.

For more on cold reading, pick up any good book dealing with body language. I would also strongly recommend the book *Dr. Abravanel's Body Type Program*, which I think can, in many ways, be more accurate than most astrology books (Bantam Books, 1985).You might also make a practice of studying people in public places—buses, trains, parks, restaurants. Study them and try to analyze them. You'll have no way of verifying your ideas but it's valuable training.

A FINAL WORD

To repeat what I said at the end of the last chapter: Don't do a cold reading unless you absolutely have to. If necessary say, "I'm sorry but I'm just not in the mood for doing a reading right now. I'll be happy to give you one later, however." Clients will respect you much more for this honesty. And . . . sincerely try to help your client, as much as you possibly can.

Don't attempt to do medical diagnoses, or prescribe medicine. You can certainly say something to the effect that "the old herbal cures were always considered very effective. Quite rightly so, to my mind." Here you are simply giving an opinion. But don't run the risk of being accused of practicing medicine without a license. Don't forget that the AMA is one of the federally encouraged monopolies!

Only read for one person at a time. You do not need an audience.

Do *disclaim* supernatural powers. Let's face it, any "powers" that you are using are in fact quite *natural*.

Dukkerin', in the Gypsy fashion, is fun, is constructive, and is essentially *practical*. None of the methods given in this book involves anything at all complicated or expensive (No, you don't *have* to have a crystal ball, if you remember!). As with so much in the parapsychological field, *practice makes perfect*. Read for everybody. Read for people you know (in this way you can verify what you see) and also for people you don't know. Drag in the mailman, the newspaperboy, the Fuller Brush man—anyone you can. Read for them (they'll probably love it!) and see how well you do.

If you need the money, or want to read professionally, don't let anyone tell you it's sinful! There is nothing wrong with being paid for a skill that you use to help others. Don't overcharge (you won't keep clients that way anyway) but don't sell yourself short either. At the same time, don't hesitate to *not* charge someone whom you feel needs a reading but cannot afford it.

The Rom are much maligned—as are the Wicca (see my *Buckland's Complete Book of Witchcraft*). *The Detroit News*, in April 1985, had a headline that screamed, "It's Gypsy Season . . . So Don't Get Gypped." As Paul Dean pointed out in a *Los Angeles Times* article (October 5, 1986), "That headline . . . would never have been published had it referred, for example, to Jews. The slur and the racism would be identical. Yet that Detroit headline inspired no public outrage, no editorial apologies or retractions." He goes on to say that the Rom remain the only ethnic minority against whom laws still operate and who are specifically named in those laws.

Gypsies are working to change this state. As Dean further reports: In 1985 ". . . the state Supreme Court ruled in favor of Gypsy fortuneteller Fatima Stevens (represented by attorney Barry Fisher) who had sued the city of Azusa claiming that its ban on fortunetellers violated her constitutional right of free speech. The ruling ended longstanding bans on fortunetelling in other South Bay cities . . . The North American Chapter of the Gypsy Lore Society has formed a Romani Anti-Defamation League."

So the Rom are fighting back and, hopefully, receiving recognition and their rights. I sincerely hope that they will be able to continue their centuries-old tradition of dukkerin', without harrassment.

Kushti bok,
Raymond Buckland

STAY IN TOUCH

BUCKLAND GYPSY FORTUNETELLING DECK
by Ray Buckland

The *Buckland Gypsy Fortunetelling Deck* is a deck of 74 cards consisting of 22 Major Arcana and 52 Minor Arcana. They are very different from the Tarot, and are a fascinating and effective tool for divination. Created by Ray Buckland, himself a Gypsy, they are authentic and realistic.

Over the past 200 years some Romani families have designed their own Major Arcana to be used with a regular deck. These new cards often bore no resemblance to the Major Arcana of the Tarot, and even varied greatly from one Gypsy family to the next.

One such Romani deck is that of the Buckland family of Gypsies, presented here for the first time ever. The *Buckland Gypsy Fortunetelling Deck* is complete. Included with the deck is a 36-page instruction book that includes all necessary information needed to use the cards. The booklet contains an introduction to the deck, the meaning of each card, the names of each Major Arcana card, and includes several original divinatory spreads.

0-87542-052-4   **(tent.) $12.95**

PRACTICAL CANDLEBURNING RITUALS
by Raymond Buckland, Ph. D.
Magick is a way in which to apply the full range of your hidden psychic powers to the problems we all face in daily life. We know that normally we use only 5% of our total powers—Magick taps powers from deep inside our psyche where we are in contact with the Universe's limitless resources.

Magick need not be complex—it can be as simple as using a few candles to focus your mind, a simple ritual to give direction to your desire, a few words to give expression to your wish. This book shows you how easy it can be. Here is magick for fun, magick as a craft, magick for success, love, luck, money, marriage, healing; magick to stop slander, to learn truth, to heal an unhappy marriage, to overcome a bad habit, to break up a love affair, etc.

Magick—with nothing fancier than ordinary candles, and the 28 rituals in this book (given in both Christian and Old Religion versions)—can transform your life. Illustrated.
0-87542-048-06, 189 pages, 5¼ x 8, softcover $5.95

PRACTICAL COLOR MAGICK
by Raymond Buckland
Raymond Buckland has produced a fascinating and useful book which shows you how to reintroduce color into your life to benefit your physical, mental and spiritual well-being!

- Learn the secret meanings of color.
- Use color to change the energy centers of your body.
- Heal yourself and others through light radiation.
- Discover the hidden aspects of your personality through color.

Practical Color Magick will teach all the powers of light and more! You'll learn new forms of expression of your innermost self, new ways of relating to others with the secret languages of light and color. Put true color back into your life with the rich spectrum of ideas and practical magical formulas.
0-87542-047-8, 136 pages, softcover, illus. $5.95

THE MAGICAL HOUSEHOLD
by Scott Cunningham and David Harrington
Whether your home is a small apartment or a palatial mansion, you want it to be something special. Now it can be with *The Magical Household*. Learn how to make your home more than just a place to live. Turn it into a place of life and fun and magic. Here you will not find the complex magic of the ceremonial magician. Rather, you will learn simple magical spells that use nothing more than items in your house: furniture, windows, doors, carpet, pets, etc. You will learn to take advantage of the *intrinsic* power and energy that is already in your home, waiting to be tapped. You will learn to make magic a part of your life. The result is a home that is safeguarded from harm and a place which will bring you happiness, health and more.
0-87542-124-5, illustrated, softcover $7.95

MAGICAL HERBALISM—The Secret Craft of the Wise
by Scott Cunningham
In *Magical Herbalism*, certain plants are prized for the special range of energies or powers they possess. This book unites the powers of plants and man to produce, and direct, change in accord with human will and desire.

This is the Magic of amulets and charms, sachets and herbal pillows, incenses and scented oils, simples and infusions and anointments. It is a magic to enjoy as we look to the Earth to rediscover our roots and make inner connections with the world of Nature.

This is the Magic of Enchantment . . . of word and gesture to shape the images of mind and channel the energies of the herbs. It is a Magic for *everyone*—for the herbs are easily and readily obtained, the tools are familiar or easily made, and the technology that of home and garden.

This book includes step-by-step guidance to the preparation of herbs and to their compounding in incense and oils, sachets and amulets, simples and infusions, with simple rituals and spells for every purpose.
0-87542-120-2, 243 pages, 5¼ x 8, illus., softcover $7.95

EARTH POWER
by Scott Cunningham

This is a book of folk magic—the magic of the common people. As such, it is different from nearly every other published work on the subject. This book is for the people of the Earth. The practices are as easy as placing a leaf in a north wind. The ritual is married to the forces of Nature. This is natural magic rediscovered.

This book can not only help you learn these natural magical methods, but it can also put you in touch with the planet that nurtures you, and gives you spells for every purpose including: weather magic, dieting, love spells, divination, meditation, protection and much more. *Earth Power* is folk magic—the magic of common people that does not need years of study, expensive paraphernalia and long rituals filled with meaningless words. Instead, it uses the *innate* magical powers of nature. Scott has uncovered magical secrets from centuries ago so that you can use them—to help yourself and loved ones—today.

0-87542-121-0, 153 pages, 5¼ x 8, illus., softcover $6.95

CHARMS, SPELLS AND FORMULAS
by Ray Malbrough

Hoodoo magick is a blend of European techniques and the magic brought to the New World by slaves from Africa. Hoodoo is a *folk magic* that can be learned and easily mastered by anyone.

By using the simple materials available in Nature, you can bring about the necessary changes to greatly benefit your life and that of your friends. You are given detailed instructions for making and using the *gris-gris* (charm) bags only casually or mysteriously mentioned by other writers. Malbrough not only shows how to make gris-gris bags for health, money, luck, love and protection from evil and harm, etc., but he also explains how these charms work. He also takes you into the world of *doll magick;* using dolls in rituals to gain love, success, or prosperity. Complete instructions are given for making the dolls and setting up the ritual.

0-87542-501-1, 192 pages, 5¼ x 8, illus., softcover $6.95

THE LLEWELLYN ANNUALS

Llewellyn's MOON SIGN BOOK: approximately 400 pages of valuable information on gardening, fishing, weather, stock market forecasts, personal horoscopes, good planting dates, and general instructions for finding the best date to do just about anything! Articles by prominent forecasters and writers in the fields of gardening, astrology, politics, economics and cycles. This special almanac, different from any other, has been published annually since 1906.

State year $3.95

Llewellyn's SUN SIGN BOOK: Your personal horoscope for the entire year! All 12 signs are included in one handy book. Lucky dates are given for many activities for each sign. Monthly horoscopes by a prominent radio and TV astrologer for your personal Sun Sign. Articles on a variety of subjects written by well-known astrologers from around the country. Much more than just a horoscope guide! Entertaining and fun the year round.

State year $3.95

Llewellyn's DAILY PLANETARY GUIDE and Astrologer's Datebook: Includes all of the major daily aspects plus their exact times in Eastern and Pacific time zones, lunar phases, signs and voids plus their times, planetary motion, a monthly ephemeris, sunrise and sunset tables, special articles on the planets, signs, aspects, a business guide, planetary hours, rulerships, and much more. Large 5¼ × 8 format for more writing space, spiral bound to lay flat, address and phone listings, time zone conversion chart and blank horoscope chart.

State year $6.95

Llewellyn's ASTROLOGICAL CALENDAR: Large wall calendar of 52 pages. Beautiful full color cover and color inside. Includes special feature articles by famous astrologers, introductory information on astrology, Lunar Gardening Guide, celestial phenomena for the year, and monthly date pages which include aspects, lunar information, planetary motion, ephemeris, personal forecasts, lucky dates, planting and fishing dates, and more. 10 x 13 size. Set in Central time, with conversion table for other time zones worldwide.

State year $6.95